BRAIN TEASERS, PUZZLES & MATHEMATICAL DIVERSIONS

Published in Great Britain by Carlton Books Limited
an imprint of the Carlton Publishing Group
20 Mortimer Street
London W1T 3JW

A catalogue record for this book is available from the British Library

ISBN 978-1-78177-183-9

Printed and bound by CPI Group (UK) Ltd, Croydon, CR0 4YY

10 9 8 7 6 5 4

BRAIN TEASERS, PUZZLES & MATHEMATICAL DIVERSIONS

ERWIN BRECHER, PhD

SEVENOAKS

ACKNOWLEDGEMENTS

Little can be achieved in any field of human endeavour without the support, encouragement and assistance of others. This book is no execption; it seemed a most formidable task when I first put pen to paper.

The puzzles have different origins; many are of my own construction, while the 'Golden Oldies' have been carefully selected to offer variety and curiosity, and to challenge the puzzle-solving capabilities of the most accomplished devotee. I am indebted to many copyright holders for permission to use material from their books. Sources include: Scot Morris, whose *Omni Games* proved to be a rich source; Martin Gardner, the doyen of puzzlists; Victor Serebriakoff and Octopus Publishing; Emerson Books Inc.; Philip Carter, Ken Russell and Sphere Books; Wide World/Tetra; *Encyclopedia Britannica*; *The Little, Brown Book of Anecdotes*; Sterling Publishing Co., Inc. 387 Park Avenue South, New York, NY 10016, for material from *The World's Best Puzzles* by Charles Barry Townsend, © 1986 Charles Barry Townsend; *The Moscow Puzzles* by Boris A. Kordemsky, edited by Martin Gardner, translated by Albert Parry (Penguin Books, 1975), © Charles Scribner's Sons, 1972; *Riddles in Mathematics* by Eugene P. Northrop; *Classic Puzzles* by Philip Carter and Ken Russell, published by Blandford Press; Christopher Maslanka, for material from *The Guardian Book of Puzzles* (Fourth Estate, 1990); Michael Holt, for material from *More Math Puzzles and Games*; Paul Sloane, for material from *Lateral Thinking Puzzles*; Pierre Berloquin for material from *Games of Logic* (HarperCollins, 1980) and Gyles Brandreth, for material from *Classic Puzzles and Word Games*. All these books are highly recommended and are a must for any puzzle library.

My thanks go go Mike Gerrard for verifying the mathematics and physics aspects of some of my puzzles; to my son Michael, who edited the manuscript and made many valuable suggestions; to Les Smith, who rescued me from drowning in paperwork; and to Jennifer Iles, who coped with innumerable corrections and revisions.

Erwin Brecher

CONTENTS

FOREWORD

Erwin Brecher's book is a fascinating collection of old and new brain teasers covering the whole spectrum of this challenging field but avoiding repetitions and trick questions so often found in puzzle literature.

A particularly attractive feature is the author's approach to presenting soutions. Not only does he describe a novel technique to solve a specific type of geometrical problem, which he calls the Zero Option, but he also guides the reader through the thought process leading to the solution. This is a welcome change to many puzzle books which simply state the answer, leaving the reader baffled as to how the solution was arrived at and more than a little frustrated at being unable to connect. This is a valuable addition to any puzzle library

Victor Serebriakoff, 1912–2000
Former Hon. President of International Mensa

INTRODUCTION

Mathematics, rightly viewed, possesses not only truth, but supreme beauty – a beauty, cold and austere, like that of a sculpture.

– Bertrand Russell (1872–1970), *Mysticism and Logic*

This book is not intended for serious mathematicians. we will not be discussing diophantine equations, fibonacci numbers or the Fermat theorems. Rather, it is written and compiled as entertainment for people who enjoy putting their mental agility to the test, a hobby gaining in popularity to judge from the growing number of periodicals that carry regular puzzle features alongside their chess, crossword and bridge columns.

Over sixty years of puzzle-solving, I have developed a prejudice in favour of puzzles persented as simply as possible and against unnecessary embellishment. I have imposed that prejudice on my readers. In these pages, you will not be meeting too many kings, queens or knaves, or journeying to mythical lands in search of dragons.

Erwin Brecher, PhD

GENERAL PUZZLES

1. THE HEIR

The king dies and two men, the true heir and an impostor, both claim to be his long-lost son. Both fit the description of the rightful heir: about the right age, height, colouring and general appearance. Finally, one of the elders proposes a test to identify the true heir. One man agrees to the test while the other flatly refuses. The one who agreed is immediately sent on his way, and the one who refused is correctly identified as the rightful heir. Why?

2. DEATH IN THE CAR

A man was shot to death while in his car. There were no powder marks on his clothing, which indicated that the gunman was outside the car. However, all the windows were up and the doors locked. After a close inspection was made, the only bullet-holes discovered were on the man's body. How was he murdered?

3. A SOLDIER'S DREAM

A soldier dreamed that his king would be assassinated on his first visit to a foreign city. He pleaded with the king to cancel the forthcoming trip, believing the dream might be a terrible omen. Pondering a moment, the king thanked the soldier for his advice and confirmed that he intended to take it, then ordered the soldier's execution. Why?

4. THE JUDGMENT

A man is found guilty of murder. The judge says, "This is one of the most vicious criminal acts that has ever come before me and I am satisfied beyond any doubt that there are no mitigating factors. I wish I could impose the stiffest sentence at my disposal, but I have no choice but to let you go." What is the reason for the judge's decision?

5. THE JILTED BRIDE

In a mountain village in Switzerland, during the winter of 1693, a couple were being married. In the midst of the ceremony, a girl, jilted by the bridegroom, appeared and made a scene.

"The wedding bell will not ring," she said, before taking poison in front of the gathering.

Sure enough, when the bellringer tried, there was no sound from the bell. Most of the celebrants assumed she had bound the clapper in some way, though a few suggested that the girl was known to be a witch and had probably cast a spell.

After the ceremony, the bellringer climbed up to the belfry to investigate, but found everything in working order.

Was the girl a witch, after all?

6. CRAFTY CABBY

In his book Aha! Insight, master gamesman Martin Gardner tells the story of a talkative, highly-strung woman who hailed a taxicab in New York City. During the journey the lady talked so much that the taxi driver got quite annoyed. He said, "I'm sorry, lady, but I can't hear a word you're saying. I'm deaf as a post, and the battery in my hearing aid is dead." This shut the woman up, but after she left the cab she figured out he had been lying to her. How did she know?

7. THE SHARPSHOOTER

A sharpshooter hung up his hat and put on a blindfold. He then walked 100 metres, turned around, and shot a bullet through his hat. The blindfold was a perfectly good one, completely blocking the man's vision. How did he manage this feat?

8. DEATH IN SQUAW VALLEY

A New York banker and his wife took their annual skiing holiday in the Valley. Late one afternoon, in bad visibility, the wife skidded over a precipice and broke her neck. The coroner returned a verdict of accidental death and released the body for burial.

In New York an airline clerk read about the accident. He contacted the police and gave them some information which resulted in the husband's arrest and indictment for first-degree murder. The clerk did not know the banker or his wife, and had never been to Squaw Valley.

What information did he give the police?

9. BURGLARS

Arthur lives with his parents in Chicago. Last week, while his parents were out, Arthur's next-door neighbour Sophie came round to spend the evening. At one point, she popped out to buy some cigarettes. Just then, two men burst into the apartment and, ignoring Arthur, took the TV set, the stereo and a computer. Arthur had never seen the men before, and they had no legal right to remove the equipment, yet he did nothing to stop them. In fact, he didn't even act surprised by their behaviour. Why not?

10. INSOMNIA

IBM executives held a sales conference at a hotel in Miami. Pete and Dave occupied adjoining rooms. After a strenuous day of presentations and partying, they went to their rooms. Despite being exhausted, Pete just could not get off to sleep. Eventually, at about two in the morning, he called the switchboard and asked to be put through to Dave's room. As soon as Dave picked up the phone, Pete replaced his and fell asleep. Explain.

11. THE NORTH POLE

Porto Allegre in Brazil is situated at longitude 50° west and latitude 30° south, at a distance of approximately 15,000 kilometres from the North Pole. Eucla in Australia is also 15,000 kilometres from the North Pole.

What are the odds that Eucla, or for that matter any other spot on Earth equally distant from the North Pole, is more than 15,000 kilometres from Porto Allegre?

12. THE LONG DIVISION

Solve the following sequence of divisions.

What is one-half of two-thirds of three-quarters of four-fifths of five-sixths of six-sevenths of seven-eighths of eight-ninths of nine-tenths of one hundred?

To find the solution without getting tied in knots you need a flash of inspiration.

13. POOL RESOURCES

Brothers Andrew and Jim had just received their weekly pocket money, and planned to go to the fairground for Sunday afternoon. Jim, suspecting a smaller allowance, suggested to Andrew that they should pool and share their cash equally. "OK," said Andrew, "I know how much you have. If you guess how much I have I will split with you. To help you out, I will give you the following clue: if you give me £1, I shall have twice as much as you; if instead I give you £1 we shall each have the same amount." How much pocket money has each brother received?

14. THE PARKING DODGE NO. 1

Clive Gordon is a paragon of virtue. He does not smoke, does not drink, pays his taxes punctually and never exceeds the prescribed speed limits. There is however one quirk in this virtuous landscape of Clive's character. He hates traffic wardens and what they stand for and he considers all parking restrictions to be an abuse of power by oppressive and faceless authorities.

A great deal of his time is devoted to devising schemes which will enable him to park wherever he wants and yet escape the scourge of parking tickets, clamping and being towed away.

One of his latest exploits is worth recording: a few months ago he took his Jaguar XJ6 to the Continent and on his way to Vienna he stopped over in Zurich for a meeting with Dr. Hans Gruber, his Swiss lawyer. He parked his car in the Talstrasse and after a brisk 5 minute walk arrived at Gruber's office. One hour later they had finished their business and when they shook hands Clive mentioned, by the way, where his car was parked.

Gruber (with a worried expression):

"You will be in serious trouble, parking in the Talstrasse is strictly limited to 20 minutes and penalties for exceeding it are very severe."

Gordon: "Don't worry, I will not be affected. However in the unlikely event that I will need your help, I shall let you know."

What devilish scheme did he have in mind?

15. THE PARKING DODGE NO. 2

After trying for weeks Clive Gordon managed to get two tickets for Sunset Boulevard at the Adelphi Theatre on the Strand. Traffic was heavy and he arrived at the theatre with only minutes to spare.

He had no time nor the inclination to look for a garage. He parked the car at a meter, which he did not even bother to feed, although it was already on excess.

He had no disabled badge and yet he knew he would not get a ticket. How did he manage it?

16. THE BLIP

After the invasion of Kuwait by Iraqi forces followed by Desert Storm, the coalition armies established their headquarters in Riyadh.

The basement of the Saudi air force building served as an intelligence gathering centre monitored by American and British personnel recruited from the CIA and MI5.

Every morning between 5:30 a.m. and 6 a.m. two of them went to a small windowless room in the basement and waited for a transmission from one of their agents which the CIA had infiltrated into Baghdad.

At precisely 5:40 a.m. they heard a single blip, lasting less than half a second. Nevertheless the blip contained an important message causing great excitement.

Furthermore the recipients were satisfied that the information was genuine, not sent by an impostor and that their agent had not sent it under duress.

Can you explain this extraordinary phenomenon?

17. A WARTIME MYSTERY

The year was 1941 and the place the headquarters of the Red Army high command, facing the Kremlin.

It was one of the hottest June days on record in Moscow and, air-conditioning being out of action, all windows in the conference room on the tenth floor were wide open.

Gregory Topolev, Chief of Staff, was reporting to the assembled top brass on routine organizational matters, when suddenly the door opened to admit the head of the KGB, accompanied by a middle-aged civilian.

Topolev took one look at them, paled, and jumped out of the window. Considering that he knew both men very well and in fact considered them his friends, how do you explain his suicide?

18. THE BLACK FOREST

Susan and Tom were tracking the Black Forest, the highland in south west Germany, when they discovered a young man hanging from a tree. Their first impulse was to cut him down, but as he was obviously dead they decided to report the find to the police.

On examination it was found that the man had died about 3 days before he was discovered, and that it was neither suicide nor murder.

What do you think had happened?

19. THE CABIN IN THE WOODS

There is an old German fairytale of two children, Hansel and Gretel, taking a stroll into the nearby woods and suddenly discovering a log cabin covered with mouth-watering sweets, the home of a wicked witch.

Our story is also about Hansel and Gretel, members of the village constabulary, who were ordered to search the forest which surrounded the neighbourhood. They too came upon a cabin, but to their horror found it full of dead men, women and children. They did not die of natural causes and no crime was involved.

What do you think had happened?

20. THE SIXPACK

It was a hot, humid summer afternoon in East Finchley. George was carrying a sixpack of Coca-Cola, bought at the local supermarket, to stock up the fridge in his home more than a mile away.

The sixpack felt like a ton and although he changed the load from left to right hand in short intervals the burden became heavier by the minute.

Suddenly an idea struck him. If he were to drink three of the cans it would not only quench his thirst, but he would have much less to carry.

Do you agree with his reasoning?

21. THE GAMBLERS

They knew it had to stop. Since his retirement Ian and Emma, his wife, had started to gamble. Initially it was out of boredom but before long they became addicted. Ian's poison was chemin de fer and Emma loved blackjack. Ian enjoyed a good pension and had substantial savings which enabled them to indulge in their favourite pastime not only in Las Vegas and Atlantic City but also in the fashionable watering holes of Monte Carlo and Deauville.

One morning, having gambled all night, they did some accounts and discovered that in a few months they had lost a fortune. They panicked and decided to join Gamblers Anonymous.

As a last fling they booked a suite near a casino for a seven-day stay. As fate would have it they won a five figure amount during the first three days. As invariably happens, they made friends with gamblers at the same tables and in the intervals, over drinks, exchanged pleasantries and gambling anecdotes.

On the fourth day something happened, as a result of which Ian and Emma, and some of their new found friends, though not all, died a slow death. No crime or disease was involved.

What do you think had happened?

22. SPIRIT OF ST. LOUIS

Charles Lindbergh's dramatic solo flight from New York to Paris in May 1927 has become part of aviation history. The Spirit of St. Louis was a single-engine plane. The flight took 33½ hours and the engine performed perfectly although it had not been tested nonstop for such a period of time. There was the risk of engine failure and the question you are asked to consider is this:

If the plane had been powered by two identical engines made by the same manufacturer and assuming that engineering technology was not sufficiently advanced to enable the plane to maintain flight on a single engine if one had failed, would Lindbergh have been safer or less safe with a twin-engine plane, or would it have made no difference?

23. THE APPOINTMENT

Gerry had at last been offered a job as a barman in one of the most exclusive establishments in San Diego. He was to attend an interview with the manager at noon.

He set off from Los Angeles at 9 a.m., in ample time for the 124-mile trip, as he had decided to travel by car, which should not take more than two hours on Highway 101.

Although there was no breakdown, no accident, and traffic was light, he arrived three hours late for his appointment and failed to get the job.

Why did it take him five hours to travel from L.A. to San Diego?

24. THE TELEPHONE CALL

A telephone conversation:

"Hello. Is this XYZ 8765?"

"Yes. Who's that?"

"What? You don't recognize my voice? Why, my mother is your mother's mother-in-law."

What is the relationship of the speakers?

25. RELATIONS

"Jean is my niece," said Jack to his sister Jill. "She is not my niece," said Jill. Can you provide more than one possible explanation?

26. SISTERS

Two look-alike girls sitting on a park bench are approached by a stranger. "You must be twins," he says.

The girls smile. "We have the same parents and were born on the same day in the same year, but, no, we're not twins."

How come?

27. HOW CLOSE?

What is the closest relation that your mother's sister-in-law's brother-in-law could be to you?

28. THE PAINTING

A man, looking at a painting, says to himself: "Brothers and sisters have I none, but that man's father is my father's son." Who is the subject of the painting?

29. SONS' AGES

Two men, both the same age, sitting in a laundromat waiting for their washes to finish, struck up a conversation. One said to the other: "I have three sons. Let's see how many clues I have to give you before you're able to work out their ages. To make it easy, we'll deal in whole years only. The question is: what are their ages next birthday?"

The other man agreed to give it a try.

The first man continued.

"One: the sum of my sons' ages is 13."

The second man shook his head.

"Two: the product of their ages is the same as your age."

"Carry on," said the second man.

"Three: my oldest son weighs 91 pounds. Four—?"

"Stop," said the second man. "I think I've got it."

What was his solution?

30. FATHER AND GRANDFATHER

Is it possible for one's grandfather to be younger than one's father?

31. FOUR FAMILIES

Every Saturday, a gang of us play some kids from Brooklyn at baseball, but the other day, because of the flu, it looked like we'd have to miss a game. Then Chuck pointed out that, because some of us were better players than the rest, we'd still be able to pull together two evenly matched teams, though it would mean mixing up the two groups.

As I was getting ready to go to bat, who should walk up but the guy who's running for Mayor this year, saying we kids all looked so cute we could be brothers and sisters.

He patted my head for the benefit of the TV crew with him, so I told him we might look alike, but actually we belonged to four different families.

"There's my family," I explained. "Ours is the largest. Then there's the Browns, they're a smaller family. The Greens are smaller still, and the Black family is the smallest of all."

He wanted to know how many kids there were in each family, but I was in the mood to be difficult, so I told him, as it happens, you could multiply together the numbers of kids in each family and come out with the same number as was the number of fools who were going to vote for him this coming November. Then I told him how many votes I reckoned he'd get!

That should have been enough to persuade him to take a hike, but instead he said: "Well, let me see if I can work out the number of children in each family." After a moment, he said: "Tell me one thing, sonny: do the Blacks have more than one child?"

I didn't see how knowing that would help him much, so I answered. But I figured I'd outfox him by just saying Yes or No. Then the wiseguy looked straight at the TV cameras and announced how many kids each family had!

How did I answer his question, and what did the wiseguy say?

(For the baseball-ignorant: there are 9 players on a team.)

32. HUSBANDS AND FATHERS

Mary and Joan run into each other quite regularly at the local supermarket. One day, Mary mentioned: "You know, the other night I was suddenly struck by the odd way in which we're related. You realize, don't you, that our fathers are our husbands, as well as the fathers of our children?" Explain.

33. HOW MANY CHILDREN?

Each son in the Hubbard family has just as many brothers as sisters, but each daughter has twice as many brothers as sisters. How many boys and girls are there in the family?

34. BOYS AND GIRLS

A sultan wanted to increase the proportion of women to men in the population of his country so that the men could have larger harems. He proposed to accomplish this by passing a law which forbade a woman to have any more children as soon as she had given birth to a male child. Thus, he reasoned, some families would have several girls and only one boy, but no family could have more than one boy. After a time, females would outnumber males. Or would they?

(In the real world, slightly more than 50 percent of births are girls, but assume that, in the sultan's country, the natural birth ratio is exactly 50-50.)

35. TWO CHILDREN

I have two children. At least one of them is a boy. What is the probability that both my children are boys?

My sister also has two children. The older child is a girl. What is the probability that both her children are girls?

36. MARITAL PROBLEM

Jason and Dean were brothers. Jason married Jackie, and Dean married Denise. However, Jason and Denise have the same wedding anniversary. Dean's wedding anniversary was one month before this date, and Jackie's was one month after it. There have been no divorces or remarriages. How do you explain this?

37. RAILWAYS

The rails in the American and British railway systems have a length of 60 feet, while most of the railways in continental Europe use sections of 30 metres (98 feet 5 inches).

You will notice that railway tracks have a small gap between adjoining sections. Why?

38. RICE AND SALT

In some countries, it is the custom to put rice in salt dispensers. Why?

39. COAL AND LIME

In some European countries, if coal is transported in open railway wagons the top is sprayed with a solution of lime. Why?

40. SAND ON THE BEACH

Walk along a beach at low tide when the sand is firm and wet. At each step the sand immediately around your foot dries out and turns white. Why? The popular answer, that your weight "squeezes the water out," is incorrect: sand doesn't behave like a sponge. So what does cause the whitening?

41. BRIDGE CLEARANCE

A trucker wants to drive under a bridge but finds that his rig is an inch higher than the bridge's clearance. The frustrated driver pulls to the side of the road and is checking maps to find his shortest alternative route when a small child comes up to him and says, "Hey, Mister, for five bucks I'll tell you how to get your truck through." Her suggestion worked. What was it?

42. A FLAT TYRE

A man whose car suddenly blows a tyre pulls up at the side of the road. He jacks up the car, removes the hubcap and 4 lug nuts, places the nuts in the hubcap, and removes the flat. As he is lifting the spare wheel out of the boot, however, he kicks over the hubcap and all the nuts fall into a drain. The next town is several miles away. Of course, he could walk or hitchhike there to buy more lug nuts, but can you think of anything better?

43. THE BIOLOGY EXAM

Scot Morris, in *The Next Book of Omni Games*, relates the story of a biology final exam:

The professor warned the students that everyone had to stop writing when the 3 o'clock bell rang, but one young man ignored him and continued writing for a few seconds more. When he dropped his exam booklet on top of the others, the professor picked it up and handed it back. "You were told to stop writing when the bell rang. Since you disobeyed, you fail the course."

The student demanded indignantly, "Do you know who I am?" "No, and furthermore, I don't care," the teacher replied. What did the student do to avoid failing the test?

44. THE MANHOLE

Why are manhole covers circular rather than square?

45. WET ROOF

When rain falls straight down onto a roof with a 45° tilt (as illustrated below), there is less rain per unit area than if the roof were level (below right). It would therefore seem that rain falling vertically on level ground would give it more of a wetting than the same rain would if it fell at an angle because of the wind. Why is this not the case?

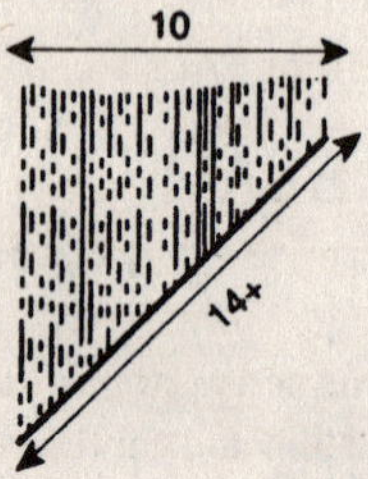

46. INNER SPACE

Down in a deep coal mine, a mile or so below the surface of the Earth, is there more gravity or less gravity than there is at the entrance to the mine up at ground level? (Assume the Earth has a uniform density, and ignore any centrifugal and centripetal forces.)

47. WEIGH-IN

Even if you stand perfectly still on an accurate scale, the reading keeps oscillating around your average weight. Why?

48. THE RIFLE

A man holds a rifle horizontally 2 metres above the ground. At the moment he fires it, another bullet is dropped from the same height, 2 metres. Ignoring frictional effects and the curvature of the Earth, which bullet hits the ground first?

49. CRACKED UP

Pour hot water into a thick drinking glass and into a thin wine glass. Which glass is more likely to crack?

50. ROLL OFF

A ball, a disc and a ring, each 12cm in diameter, sit at the top of an inclined plane. If all three objects start rolling down the incline at the same instant, which one will reach the bottom first? (Assume that they all roll efficiently—that is, they are perfectly formed and don't wobble—and ignore any effect of air resistance and friction.)

51. MOUNTAIN TIME

If you take your mechanical watch to the mountains, will it run faster or more slowly than usual?

52. LAUNCH PADS

Why are space centres like Cape Canaveral usually located in tropical climates?

53. POLES APART

Antarctica has 8 times as much ice as the Arctic. Why is there so much more ice at the South Pole than there is at the North?

54. A HARD SKATE

Is it easier to ice skate when the air temperature is at minus 15°C or at minus 1°C?

55. THE SUSPENDED EGG

How would you make a raw egg float halfway between the surface and the bottom of a glass of water?

56. TWO BARS OF IRON

Two bars of iron lie on a table. They look identical, but one of them is magnetized (with a pole at each end), the other is not.

How can you discover which bar is magnetized if you are only allowed to shift them on the table, without raising them and without the help of any other object or instrument?

57. THE BIRD CAGE

A cage with a bird in it, perched on a swing, weighs 2 kg. Is the weight of the cage less if the bird is flying about the cage instead of sitting on the swing? Ignoring the fact that if left in an airtight box for long the bird would die, would the answer be different if an airtight box were substituted for the cage?

58. EXCEPTION TO THE RULE

It is generally accepted that matter expands with increasing temperature, and contracts with decreasing temperature. There is one notable exception. What is it, and why has nature provided for it?

59. WATER LEVEL PROBLEM

An ice cube is floating in a beaker of water, with the entire system at 0° Centigrade. Just enough heat is applied to melt the ice cube without raising the temperature of the system. What happens to the water level in the beaker? Does it rise, fall, or stay the same?

60. BOAT IN THE BATH

Rupert is sailing a plastic boat in his bath. The boat is loaded with nuts, bolts and washers. If Rupert dumps all these items into the water, allowing his boat to float empty, will the water level in the bath rise or fall?

61. SPACE STATION

People have speculated that, one day in the far future, it may be possible to hollow out the interior of a large asteroid or moon and use it as a permanent space station. Assuming that such a hollowed-out asteroid is a perfect, non-rotating sphere with an outside shell of constant thickness, would an object inside, near the shell, be pulled by the shell's gravity field towards the shell or towards the centre of the asteroid, or would it float permanently at the same location?

62. BIRD ON THE MOON

Imagine a bird with a small, lightweight oxygen tank attached to its back so that it can breathe on the moon. Given that the pull of gravity is less than on Earth, will the bird's flying speed on the moon be faster, slower, or the same as its speed on the Earth? Assume that, for the purposes of making the comparison, the bird has to carry the same equipment on Earth.

63. THE GOLDFISH

A goldfish bowl, three-quarters full of water, is placed on a weighing scale. If a live goldfish is dropped into the water, the scale will show an increase in weight equal to the weight of the fish. However, assume that the goldfish is held by its tail so that all but the extreme tip of its tail is under water. Will this operation cause the scale to register a greater weight than it did before the fish was suspended?

64. SPEED OF SOUND

The speed of sound in air is about 740 miles per hour. Suppose that a police car is sounding its siren and is driving towards you at 60 miles per hour. At what speed is the sound of the siren approaching you?

65. TWO BRIDGES

Imagine two bridges that are exactly alike except that every dimension in one is twice as large as in the other. For example, the large bridge is two times longer, its structural members are two times thicker, and so forth. Which bridge is stronger, or is their strength the same?

66. TWO SAILBOATS

Imagine two sailboats built to exactly the same proportions except that one is twice as large as the other: its masts are twice as thick; its sails are twice as long and twice as wide. Even though the sails are made out of the same kind of canvas, if the weight of the sail itself can be ignored, which sailboat will be more likely to have its sail torn by the force of the wind?

67. AIRCRAFT TEMPERATURE

When an airliner is flying at an altitude of 30,000 feet, the temperature of the air outside may be as low as -35°C. One might think that this would require the use of heaters inside the cabin, but in fact an aircraft flying this high must use air-conditioners. Why?

68. FAN POWER

You wanted to sail your model sailboat today, but there is no wind at all and your boat is in the doldrums. Would it be possible to propel your boat by mounting a battery-operated fan on the rear of the boat and directing the fan to blow wind into the sails?

69. FLAGS

Below are the flags of Pakistan (left) and Algeria (right). The flags of the Comoro Islands, Mauritania and Tunisia have similar designs. Astronomically, is there anything "wrong" with them?

70. WHERE ARE YOU?

Suppose you are a passenger in a doughnut-shaped space station. It is spinning around its hub to produce a simulated gravity of 1 g, exactly mimicking the gravity of Earth. You are in a small, windowless room, so you cannot see the rest of the space station. Inside your room everything seems "normal"—gravity seems to be operating on you exactly as it would on Earth. In fact, as far as your senses can tell you, you are on Earth.

You have a coin in your pocket. Is there a simple test you could do in your room that would confirm you are on a spinning space station and not on Earth?

71. BRIDGE TOWERS

The longest suspension bridge in the world is the Humber Estuary bridge in England, just short of 1 mile long between the supports. The two towers are not quite parallel. They are 35mm inches farther apart at the top than at the bottom. Why?

72. DROPS AND BUBBLES

If all space were empty except for two drops of water, the drops would be attracted to each other, according to Newton's Law of Gravity.

Now suppose all space were full of water except for two bubbles (see above). Would the bubbles move apart, towards each other, or not at all?

73. SPECIAL SPHERE

If a sphere 20 feet (just over 6 metres) in diameter enclosed a vacuum and weighed 300 lb (136 kg), what amazing property would it possess?

74. THE STRIKING CLOCK

It takes a clock two seconds to strike 2 o'clock. How long will it take to strike 3 o'clock?

75. RED OR GREEN

You are given 4 pieces of cardboard and told that each one is either red or green on one side, and that each one has either a circle or a square on the other side. They appear on the table as follows:

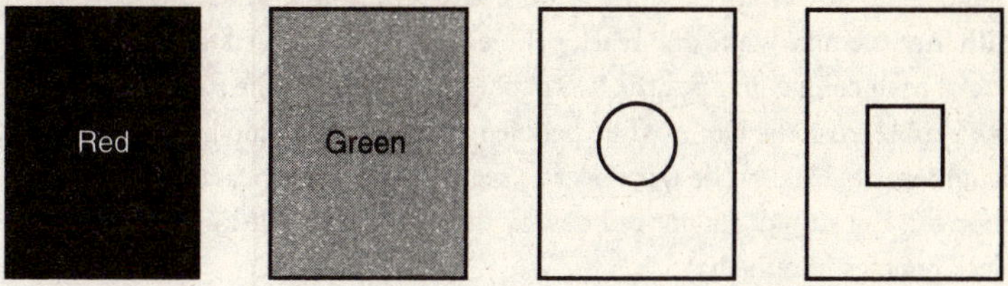

How many cards, and which ones, must you turn over in order to have sufficient information to answer the question: Does every red card have a square on its other side?

76. THE RIVER

A man takes his motor boat down a river to his pub. Going with the current he can cover the 2 km in 4 minutes. Returning against the current, which is steady, it takes him 8 minutes. How long does it take him at still water, when there is no current?

77. CHANGING THE ODDS

In a distant kingdom lived a king who had a beautiful daughter. She fell in love with a humble peasant boy, whom she wanted to marry. The king, who had no intention of consenting to the marriage, suggested that the decision be left to chance. The three were standing in the castle's forecourt, which was covered with innumerable white and black pebbles. The king claimed to have picked up one of each colour, and put the two pebbles into his hat. The suitor had to pick one pebble from the hat. A white pebble meant that he could marry the king's daughter; a black, that he was never to see her again. The peasant boy was poor, but not stupid. He noticed that by sleight of hand, the king had put two black pebbles into the hat.

How did the suitor resolve his predicament without calling the king a cheat?

78. ZENO'S PARADOX

In the fifth century B.C., Zeno, using his knowledge of infinity, sequences and partial sums, developed this famous paradox. He proposed that, in a race with Achilles, the tortoise be given a head start of 1,000 metres. Assume that Achilles could run 10 times faster than the tortoise. When the race started and Achilles had gone 1,000 metres, the tortoise would still be 100 metres ahead. When Achilles had gone the next 100 metres the tortoise would be 10 metres ahead. Zeno argued that Achilles would constantly gain on the tortoise, but he would never reach him. Was his reasoning correct? If Achilles were to pass the tortoise, at what point of the race would it be?

79. THE BOY AND THE GIRL

A boy and a girl are talking.

"I'm a boy," says the one with black hair. "I'm a girl," says the one with red hair.

If at least one of them is lying, which is which?

80. INFINITY AND LIMITS

The figure below illustrates circumscribing regular polygons. The number of sides of the polygon successively increases. Will the radii grow without limit? If not, can you estimate the limit, assuming the smallest circle to have a radius of 1 centimetre?

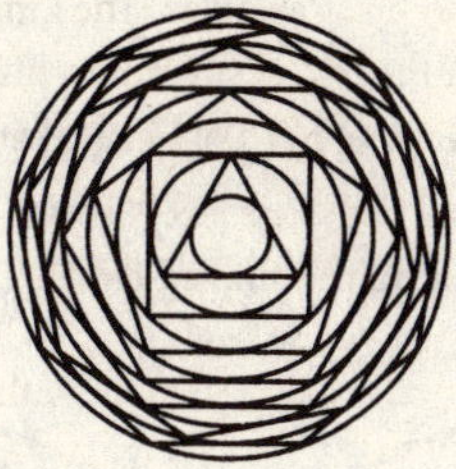

81. HATS IN THE WIND

Ten people, all wearing hats, were walking along a street when a sudden wind blew their hats off. A helpful boy retrieved them and, without asking which hat belonged to which person, handed each person a hat. What is the probability that exactly 9 of the people received their own hats?

82. HANDSHAKES

Is the number of people in the world who have shaken hands with an odd number of people odd or even?

83. MOVE ONE

The following equation, in Roman numerals, suggests that 6 plus 2 equal 5. Can you correct it by moving only one line?

VI + II = V

84. A CHIMING CLOCK

A clock chimes every hour on the hour, and once each quarter hour in between. If you hear it chime once, what is the longest you may have to wait to be sure what time it is?

85. RING AROUND THE CIRCLE

The three circles below are all the same size. How many circles will it take in all to make a complete ring around the shaded circle? Do this one without using coins or other circles, and prove your answer.

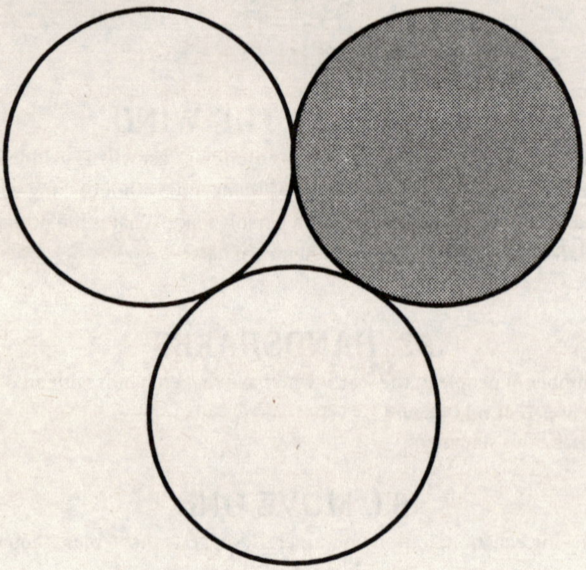

86. A UNIQUE NUMBER

The following number is the only one of its kind. Can you figure out what is so special about it?

8,549,176,320

87. THE BOSS AND HIS CHAUFFEUR

A chauffeur always arrives at the train station at exactly 5 o'clock to pick up his boss and drive him home. One day, his boss arrives an hour early, starts walking home, and is eventually picked up. He arrives home 20 minutes earlier than usual. How long did he walk before he met his chauffeur?

88. WEATHER REPORT

"Can you tell me what the temperature has been at noon for the past five days?" John asked the weatherman.

"I don't exactly recall," replied the weatherman, "but I do remember that the temperature was different each day, and that the product of the temperatures is 12."

Assuming that the temperatures are expressed to the nearest degree, what were the five temperatures?

89. CAN YOU?

"We eat what we can, and we can what we can't." Can you explain who could make this statement.

90. PRESIDENTS

"Here is an odd item, Professor Flugel," said Tom, looking up from his newspaper. "It says here that three of the first five presidents of the United States died on the Fourth of July. I wonder what the odds are against a coincidence like that."

"I'm not sure," replied the professor, "but I'm willing to give 10 to 1 odds I can name one of the three who died on that date."

Assuming that the professor had no prior knowledge of the dates on which any of the presidents died, was he justified in offering such odds?

91. JIM AND GEORGE

How is it possible for Jim to stand behind George and George to stand behind Jim at the same time?

92. TWO SIZES OF APPLES

A man had an apple stall and sold his larger apples at 3 for £1 and his smaller apples at 5 for £1. When he had just 30 apples of each size left to sell, he asked his son to look after the stall while he had lunch. When he came back from lunch the apples were all gone and the son gave his father £15. The father questioned his son. "You should have received £10 for the 30 large apples and £6 for the 30 small apples, making £16 in all." The son looked surprised. "I am sure I gave you all the money I received and I counted the change most carefully. It was difficult to manage without you here, and, as there was an equal number of each sized apple left, I sold them all at the average price of 4 for £1. Four into 60 goes 15 times so I am sure £15 is correct.
Where did the £1 go?

93. THE SEQUENCE

A friend asks you to continue the following sequence.

OTTFFS . . .

When this suggests nothing to you he adds another term:

OTTFFSS . . .

The pairs of letters TT, FF, SS now suggest something, but you still cannot deduce the sequence. He adds another term:

OTTFFSSE . . .

You are still worried by the initial term O, but otherwise every other pair of terms seems to run in reverse sequence through the alphabet (TT, SS, RR, QQ . . .) and (FF, EE, DD, CC . . .), so you write down

OTTFFSSEERRDD . . .

What is the real solution?

94. THE HALF-FULL BARREL

Two farmers were staring into a large barrel partly filled with ale. One of them said: “It’s over half full!” But the other declared: “It’s more than half empty.” How could they tell without using a ruler, string, bottles, or other measuring devices if it was more or less than exactly half full?

95. THE MARKSMAN

One marksman can fire 5 shots in 5 seconds while another can get off 10 shots in 10 seconds. (We will assume that timing starts when the first shot is fired and ends with the last shot, but the shots themselves will be assumed to take no time.)

Which man can fire 12 shots in a shorter time?

96. THE SQUARE TABLE

A square table is constructed with an obstruction in the middle of it, so that when 4 people are seated, one on each side, each can see his neighbours to right and left but not the person seated directly across. The 4 people seated at this table were told to raise their hands if, when looking to the right and left, they saw at least one woman. They were also told to announce the sex of the one person whom they could not see, if they could figure it out.

Since, as a matter of fact, all 4 people were women, each raised her hand, but then several minutes went by before one of them announced that she was certain that the person seated opposite her was a woman.

How could she logically have come to that conclusion?

97. THE MARBLES

Two bags each contain 3 red, 3 white, and 3 blue marbles. Without looking, someone removes from the first bag the largest number of marbles that it is possible to remove while still being sure that at least one of each colour remains. These marbles are put into the second bag. Now he transfers back (without looking, of course) the smallest possible number of marbles that will assure there being at least 2 of each colour in the first bag. How many marbles remain in the second bag?

98. A CARBON COPY

For some reason, probably dishonest, someone wants to write a letter that will appear to be a carbon copy. He has only one sheet of paper and one piece of carbon paper, which he places under the letter paper with the carbon side facing the back of the sheet.

He then writes with a pen which has no ink so the writing will appear only on the underside of the paper. If he wrote normally on the top of the paper (with the inkless pen) the writing would appear inverted on the underside, so he decides he will have to write invertedly. For instance, instead of the usual F, he will write ꟻ; instead of R, he will write Я.

Should he start the letter in the upper left-hand corner, upper right, lower right, or lower left?

99. WALKING IN STEP

A man and a woman, walking together, both start out by taking a step with the left foot. In order to keep together, the man, whose stride is longer, takes two steps while the woman takes three.

How many steps will the woman have taken when they are both about to step out together with their right feet for the first time?

100. RAZOR SHORTAGE

Due to rumours that there is a world shortage, people have started hoarding packs of razors. By the time I reached the supermarket, there were no packs left. However, the two people who checked out ahead of me had bought 3 packs and 5 packs respectively, and they offered to share them with me so that we each took home the same number of razors. I paid them £8. How did they divide the £8?

101. UNUSUAL EQUATIONS

$$5 + 5 + 5 = 550$$

a) Using a line the size of a hyphen, i.e. a - in any position, rectify the above equation.

b) Using four nines, make them equal 100.
c) Do the same with four sevens.
d) Arrange three nines to equal 20.

102. THE D'ALEMBERT PARADOX

The French mathematician d'Alembert (1717-83) considered the probability of throwing heads at least once when tossing a coin twice. "There are only three possible cases," he argued, "(a) Tails appears on the first toss and again on the second toss, (b) Tails appears on the first toss and heads on the second toss, (c) Heads appears on the first toss (therefore in this case there is no longer any need to carry out the second toss)."

"It is quite simple," he stated, "because there are only three possible cases; and as two of these are favourable, the probability is 2/3." Was his reasoning correct?

103. JUGS

There are many variations of puzzles involving decanting (pouring from one container to another). The one presented here is known to be at least 400 years old.

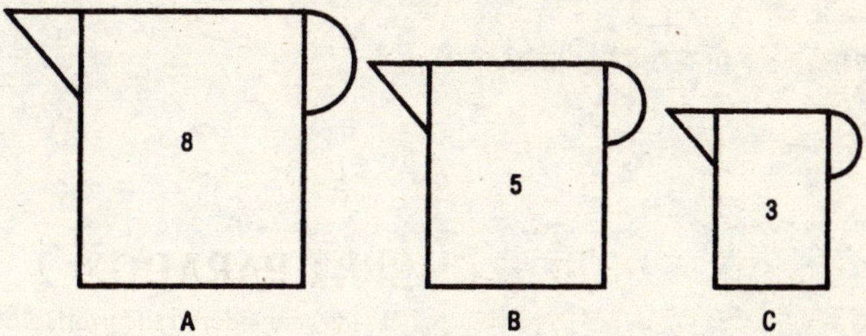

Three jugs (above) have capacity for 8, 5 and 3 litres respectively. The 8-litre jug is filled entirely with water and the other two jugs are empty. Your task is, by decanting, to divide the water into two equal parts, i.e. 4 litres in jug A and 4 litres in jug B, leaving the smallest jug empty. None of the jugs is calibrated, so the only way the task can be successfully performed is to pour water from one jug to another until the first jug is entirely empty or the second jug is entirely full. You must assume that the decanting is done with great care so that no water is spilled. What is the least number of decantings in which the task can be achieved?

104. ONE-TWO-THREE

I first heard this puzzle from a Mensa member who had come across it years before at a mathematical conference in Holland. I gave the puzzle to a friend of mine who could not solve it and took it along to his club. The members there pondered over it for many hours without success. Finally, one member took it home to show his 12-year-old son, who solved it in 5 minutes. It is that type of puzzle.

What is the next row of digits?

```
1
1 1
2 1
1 2 1 1
1 1 1 2 2 1
3 1 2 2 1 1
1 3 1 1 2 2 2 1
1 1 1 3 2 1 3 2 1 1
? ? ? ? ? ? ? ? ? ?
```

105. A BOTTLE OF WINE

A bottle of wine costs £10. If the wine is worth £9 more than the bottle, what is the value of the bottle?

106. ROLL-A-PENNY

We all remember the old fairground game which is still to be found, "Roll-a-Penny," in which the penny has to come to rest clear of any of the crossed lines.

How does one calculate the chances of winning?

Here is an example of a typical linoleum-topped table on which the game is played. How much better are the odds for the "house" than for the punter?

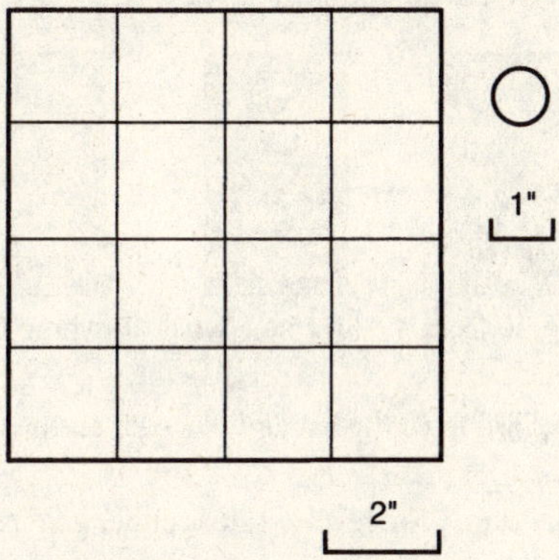

107. THE MISSING £

This is a very old English puzzle. Three men dined in a restaurant and the bill came to £25.

Each man gave the waiter £10 and told him to keep £2 out of the change as a tip.

The waiter returned with £3 and proceeded to give each man £1.

The meal had therefore cost £27 plus £2 for the waiter's tip. Where had the other £1 gone?

108. GOLD CARD

This puzzle was a favourite of Wild West card-sharps, who won thousands of dollars from the unsuspecting gold prospectors. In a saloon, the gambler would gather a crowd and place 3 cards into a hat. These cards were coloured:

GOLD on one side, GOLD on reverse;
SILVER on one side, SILVER on reverse;
GOLD on one side, SILVER on reverse.

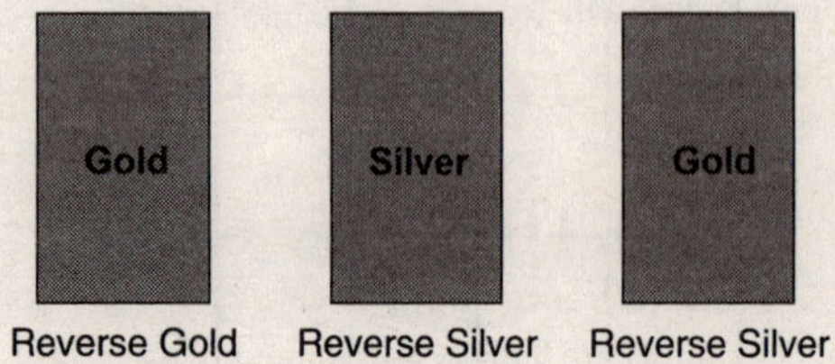

The gambler drew a card from the hat and placed it on the table with a Gold side up.

Then the gambler said: "The reverse side is either gold or silver as the card cannot be the silver/silver card. Therefore it is either the gold/silver card or the gold/gold card, an even chance! I will bet even money one dollar that the reverse side is gold." Is this a fair bet?

109. THE AEROPLANE

A plane flies in a straight line from airport A to airport B, then back in a straight line from B to A. It travels with a constant engine speed and there is no wind. Will its travel time for the same round trip be greater, less or the same if, throughout both flights, at the same engine speed, a constant wind blows from A to B?

110. SKIING THE GLOBE

The members of a water-skiing club, based in Long Beach, want to try the first circumnavigation of the globe, via the Capes and the Timor Sea, by a water skier. Aside from all other difficulties associated with this feat, they have a problem in that the best speedboats can only carry enough fuel to get half-way around—though they are able to transfer fuel from one boat to another without stopping.

The task the club has set itself is to find a way to get one speedboat and a skier all the way around the Earth without stopping, while, of course, ensuring that all the support speedboats (carrying fuel supplies) return safely to Long Beach. Is this possible?

111. FOUR INSECTS

Four insects—A, B, C and D—occupy the corners of a 10cm square (see below). A and C are male, B and D are female. Simultaneously, A crawls directly towards B, B towards C, C towards D and D towards A. If all four insects crawl at the same constant rate, they will describe four congruent logarithmic spirals which meet at the centre of the square.

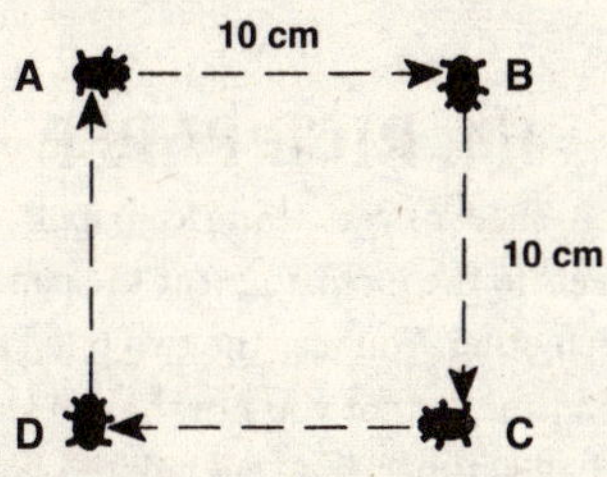

How far does each insect travel before they meet? (The problem can be solved without calculus.)

112. BIRTH DATES

You are one of 24 guests at a cocktail party and you bet a friend that there is at least one coincidence of birth dates among the people in the room. If you exclude leap years do you have a better chance of winning or losing the bet?

113. CHANGING MONEY

Here is that very puzzling story having to do with foreign exchange. The governments of two neighbouring countries—let's call them Eastland and Westland—had an agreement whereby an Eastland dollar was worth a dollar in Westland, and vice versa. But, one day, the government of Eastland decreed that thereafter a Westland dollar was to be worth only 90 cents in Eastland. The next day the Westland government, not to be outdone, decreed that thereafter an Eastland dollar was to be worth only 90 cents in Westland.

A young entrepreneur named Malcolm lived in a town which straddled the border between the two countries. He went into a shop on the Eastland side, bought a 10-cent razor, and paid for it with an Eastland dollar. He was given a Westland dollar, worth 90 cents there, in change. He then crossed the street, went into a Westland store, bought a 10-cent package of blades, and paid for it with the Westland dollar. There he was given an Eastland dollar in change. When Malcolm returned home, he had his original dollar and his purchases. And each of the tradesmen had 10 cents in his cash-drawer.

Who, then, paid for the razor and blades?

114. RICE PAPER

Suppose you have a large sheet of very thin rice paper one-thousandth of an inch thick, or 1,000 sheets to the inch. You tear the paper in half and pile the two pieces on top of each other. You tear the two piled sheets in half and stack them again, then a third time so that you now have a stack of 8 sheets, and so on. If you keep doing that 50 times, how tall will the final stack be? The usual responses are amusing. Some people suggest a foot, others go as high as several feet, a few even suggest a mile. What do you think?

115. TWO DISCS

Consider the two equal circular discs, A and B, in the figure below.

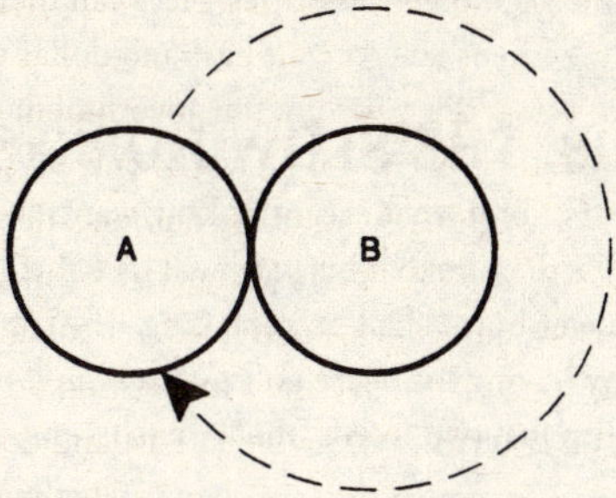

If B is kept fixed and A is rolled around B without slipping, how many revolutions will A have made about its own centre when it is back in its original position?

116. THE SLAB AND THE ROLLERS

If the circumference of each roller in the figure below is 1 metre, how far forward will the slab have moved when the rollers have made one revolution?

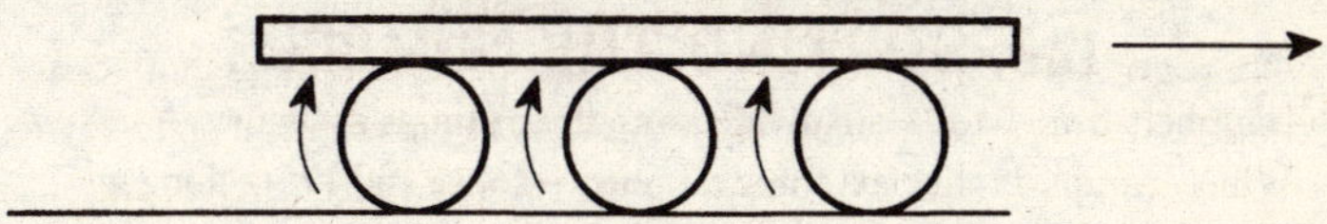

117. THE BROKEN STICK

If a stick is broken at random into 3 pieces, what is the probability that the pieces can be put together to make a triangle?

118. THE SLOW HORSES

An aged and, it appears, somewhat eccentric king wants to pass his throne on to one of his 2 sons. He decrees that his sons will race their horses and that the son who owns the slower horse shall become king. The sons, each fearing that the other will cheat by having his horse go less fast than it is capable of, ask a wise man's advice. With just two words, the wise man ensures that the race will be fair.

What does he say?

119. HOURGLASS

You have two hourglasses—a 4-minute glass and a 7-minute glass. You want to measure 9 minutes.

How do you do it?

120. SORTING THE NUMBERS

The numbers from 0 to 14 are divided into three groups as follows:

Which groups do the next three numbers—15, 16 and 17—belong in?

Group 1	*Group 2*	*Group 3*
0 3 6 8 9	1 4 7 11 14	2 5 10 12 13

121. CATEGORIES

The letters of the alphabet can be arranged in four distinct groups. The first 13 letters establish the categories:

AM
BCDEK
FGJL
HI

Place the remaining 13 letters in their proper categories.

122. WHAT WEIGHTS?

A boy selling fruit has only three weights, but with them he can weigh any whole number of kilograms from 1 kg to 13 kg inclusive. What weights does he have?

123. ROPE TRICK

Two flagpoles are each 100 feet high. A rope 150 feet long is strung between the tops of the flagpoles. At its lowest point the rope sags to within 25 feet of the ground (see figure above). How far apart are the flagpoles?

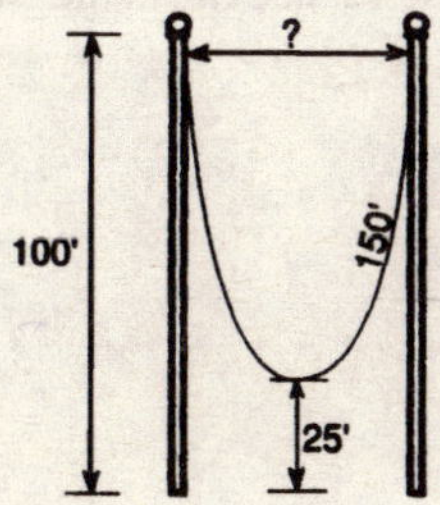

124. CATCHING THE BUS

Juliette and her sister Lucille live together in the town of Montreux in the Swiss Alps. In the springtime, one of their favourite walks is to go up to the lovely fields of narcissi growing on the mountain slopes nearby.

On one occasion they came to a long straight stretch of road, and, at a certain point on it, they left the road and walked at right angles across a field to a large clump of narcissi. Juliette stopped to pick some of the flowers 40 metres away from the road, while Lucille also collected some flowers another metre farther away. Suddenly they looked up to see a bus going along the road to Montreux. When they had decided to ride home, the bus was 70 metres away from the point where they left the road to walk across the field.

They ran at half the speed the bus travelled to the point where they left the road and missed the bus! There is at least one point on that stretch of road where the bus could have been caught.

Can you calculate where they should have run and if both of the sisters could have caught the bus?

125. BUS TIMETABLE

A man drives along a main road on which a regular service of buses is in operation. He is driving at a constant speed. He notices that every 3 minutes he meets a bus and that every 6 minutes a bus overtakes him. How often does a bus leave the terminal station at one end of the route?

126. HOW MANY HOPS?

You are standing at the centre of a circle of radius 9 feet. You begin to hop in a straight line to the circumference. Your first hop is 4½ feet, your second 2¼ feet, and you continue to hop each time half the length of your previous hop. How many hops will you make before you get out of the circle?

127. DECAFFEINÉ

This is to be solved in the head, without paper and pencil.

If some coffee is "97 percent caffeine-free," how many cups of it would one have to drink to get the amount of caffeine in a cup of regular coffee?

128. SPEED TEST

Complete this equation in less than one minute:
1234567890/12345678912 – (1234567890 × 1234567892) = ?

129. WALKING HOME

John was going home from Brighton. He went halfway by train, 15 times as fast as he goes on foot. The second half he went by ox cart. He can walk twice as fast as that.

Would he have saved time if he had gone all the way on foot? If so, how much?

130. THE WATCHMAKER

A watchmaker was telephoned to make an urgent house call to replace the broken hands of a clock. He was sick, so he sent his apprentice.

The apprentice was thorough. When he finished inspecting the clock it was dark. He hurriedly attached the new hands, but mixed up the hour and the minute hands. He then set the clock by his pocket watch. It was 6 o'clock, so he set the big hand at 6 and the little hand at 12.

The apprentice returned, but soon the telephone rang. He picked up the receiver only to hear the client's angry voice: "You didn't do the job right. The clock shows the wrong time."

Surprised, he hurried back to the client's house. He found the clock showing not much past 8. He handed his watch to the client, saying: "Check the time, please. Your clock is not off even by 1 second."

The client had to agree.

Early next morning the client telephoned to say that the clock hands, having apparently gone berserk, were moving around the clock at will. When the apprentice rushed over, the clock showed a little past 7. After checking with his watch, the apprentice got angry:

"You are making fun of me! Your clock shows the right time!"

Do you know what was going on?

131. THE LEAD PLATE

The builders of an irrigation canal needed a lead plate of a certain size, but had no lead in stock. They decided to melt some lead shot. But how could they find its volume beforehand?

One suggestion was to measure a ball, apply the formula for the volume of a sphere, and multiply by the number of balls. But this would take too long, and anyway the shot wasn't all the same size.

Another was to weigh all the shot and divide by the specific gravity of lead. Unfortunately, no one could remember this ratio, and there was no manual on the site.

Another was to pour the shot into a gallon jug. But the volume of the jug is greater than the volume of the shot by an undetermined amount, since the shot cannot be packed solid and part of the jug contains air.

Do you have a suggestion?

132. THE CALIPER

A student had to measure a cylindrical machine part with indentations at its bases (see below).

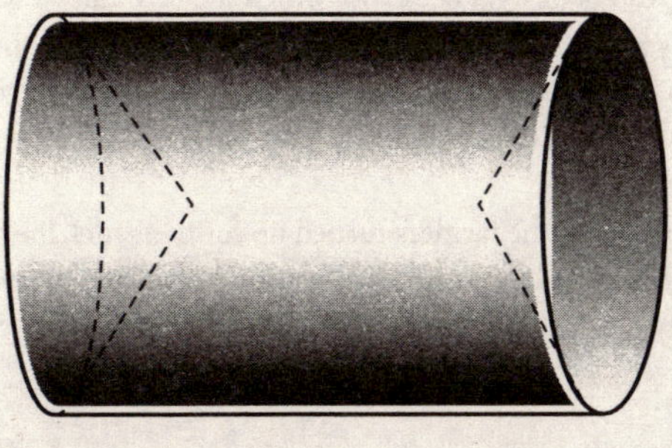

He had no depth gauge, only a caliper and a ruler. The problem was, he could find the distance between the indentations with the caliper, but he would have to remove the caliper to measure its spread on the ruler. But to remove the caliper he would have to open the legs, and then there would be nothing to measure.

What did he do?

133. FUEL TANKS

A small fuel station supplies the farms on the outskirts of town with fuel for their vehicles. It receives deliveries once a month, and stores the fuel in 6 tanks, of different sizes, reserved exclusively for the farms. Five tanks hold diesel fuel and the sixth a special blend of unleaded petrol and alcohol. The tanks are labelled to show their capacities as follows:

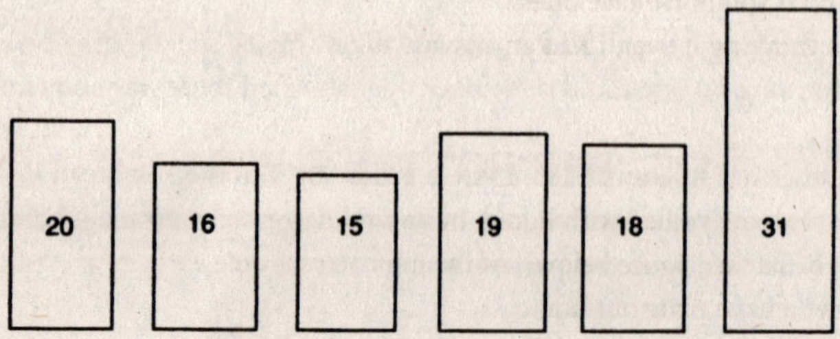

Some of the diesel is sold to Joe Smith, and the balance—exactly twice as much as Joe takes—is bought by Pete Brown's place. The unleaded/alcohol blend is for Dave Jones. Last month, all three farmers turned up together to collect their supplies, at a time when the only person working at the gas station was a new kid who hadn't yet been told which tank contained which type of fuel. Neither he nor the farmers had any means of measuring the fuel, the tanks in which the farmers carried off their supplies having larger capacities than the amount of fuel they bought each month, and not being calibrated in any way.

Nevertheless, when the farmers turned up for their fuel, the kid was able to work out which tank held the unleaded/alcohol blend and to fill the other two orders correctly.

How?

134. THE WIRE'S DIAMETER

At technical school we study the construction of lathes and machines. We learn how to use instruments and how not to be stumped by difficult situations.

My foreman-teacher handed me some wire and asked: "How do you measure a wire's diameter?"

"With a micrometer gauge."

"And if you don't have one?"

On thinking it over, I had an answer. What was it?

135. THE BOTTLE'S VOLUME

If a bottle, partly filled with liquid, has a round, square or rectangular bottom which is flat (see figure below), can you find its volume using only a rule? You may not add or pour out liquid.

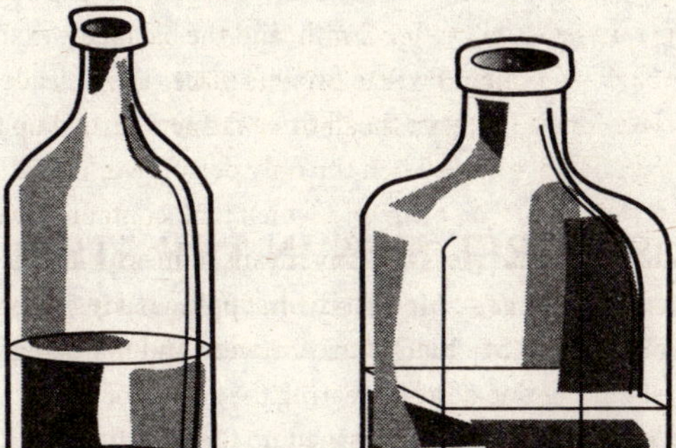

136. THE SHIP AND THE SEAPLANE

A diesel ship leaves on a long voyage. When it is 180 miles from shore, a seaplane, whose speed is 10 times that of the ship, is sent to deliver mail. How far from shore does the seaplane catch up with the ship?

137. THE SHIPS AND THE LIFEBUOY

Two diesel ships leave a pier simultaneously, the Neptune downstream and the Poseidon upstream, with the same motive force.

As they leave, a lifebuoy falls off the Neptune and floats downstream. An hour later both ships are ordered to reverse course.

Will the Neptune's crew be able to pick up the buoy before the ships meet?

138. EQUATION TO SOLVE IN YOUR HEAD

$$6{,}751x + 3{,}249y = 26{,}751$$
$$3{,}249x + 6{,}751y = 23{,}249$$

139. THREE MEN IN THE STREET

Three men met on the street—Mr. Black, Mr. Gray and Mr. White.

"Do you know," asked Mr. Black, "that between us we are wearing black, gray and white? Yet not one of us is wearing the colour of his name?"

"Why, that's right," said the man in white.

Can you say who was wearing which colour?

140. THE SQUARE FIELD

A farmer had a square field with 4 equally spaced oaks in it standing in a row from the centre to the middle of one side, as shown in the figure below.

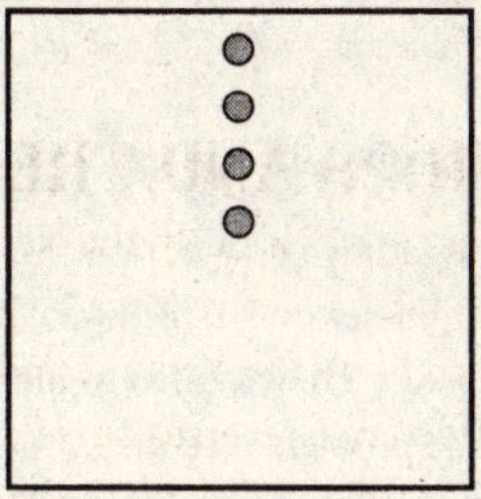

In his will, he left the square field to his 4 sons "to be divided up into 4 identical parts, each with its oak."

How did the sons divide up the land?

141. KINGS AND QUEENS

Three playing cards have been removed from an ordinary pack of cards and placed face down in a horizontal row. To the right of a King there are one or two Queens. To the left of a Queen there are one or two Queens. To the left of a Heart there are one or two Spades. To the right of a Spade there are one or two Spades.

What are the three cards?

142. EVEN TREAD

I keep one spare tyre in my car. Last year, I drove 10,000 miles in my car, and rotated the tyres at intervals so that, by the end of the year, each of the five tyres had been used for the same number of miles. For how many miles was each tyre used?

143. ROUND AND ROUND

Imagine Wheel A, with diameter x, rolling around fixed Wheel B, with diameter 2x. How many revolutions about its own axis will Wheel A make in rolling once around Wheel B?

144. CHOOSE A GLASS

Some detectives were investigating a case of poisoning at a hotel. They had lined up a number of partly filled glasses on a table in the hotel lounge, knowing that only one glass contained poison. They wanted to identify which one before testing it for fingerprints. The problem was that, if the police laboratory were asked to test the liquid in each glass, it would take too long. So the inspector in charge contacted a statistician at the local college to see if there was a quicker way. He came over to the hotel, counted the glasses, smiled, and said:

"Choose any glass, Inspector, and we'll test it first."

The inspector was worried that this would mean the waste of one test but the statistician denied this.

Later that evening, the inspector was telling his wife about the incident.

"How many glasses were there to start with?" she asked.

"I don't remember exactly—somewhere between 100 and 200 I think," replied the inspector.

Can you work out the exact number of glasses? (Assume that any group of glasses can be tested simultaneously by taking a small sample of liquid from each, mixing the samples and making a single test on the mixture.)

145. THE SQUARE WINDOW

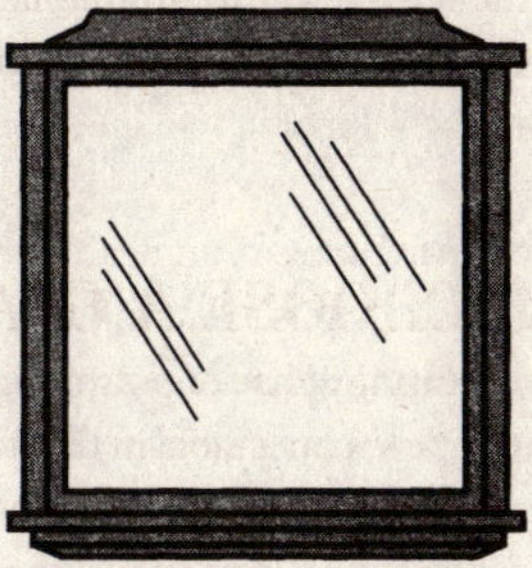

Shown above is a shop window that measures 3 metres high by 3 metres wide. The decorator wants to paint half the window blue and still have a square, clear section of window that measures 3 metres high by 3 metres wide. How would he do this?

146. DOMINOES

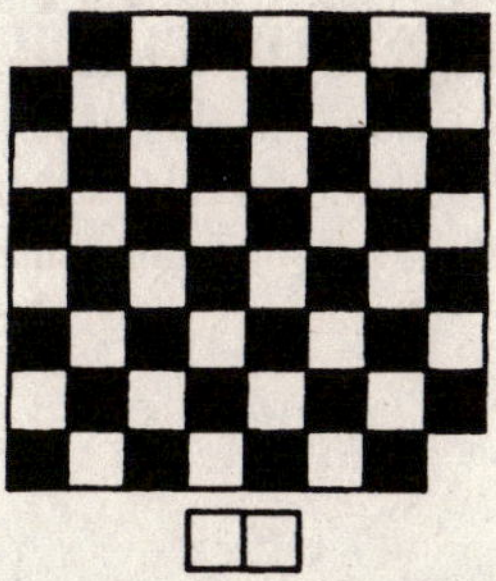

If you were challenged to cover the board with 32 dominoes, each domino exactly covering two squares on the board, you could solve it in many ways. The draughts board above has only 62 squares (two corner squares have been removed), and you must cover this board with 31 dominoes. Can you find a solution? Or if you can't, can you explain why no one ever will?

147. A BRIDGE GAME

In the game of bridge, all the cards are dealt to 4 players—13 cards to each—who usually play as partners, one pair against the other. That should be all you need to know in order to answer the following two questions about situations that might arise in a game.

FLUSH. You and your partner have been dealt a surprising hand. Together you have all 13 cards of one suit. Is this event more or less likely than one in which you and your partner together have no cards in one of the suits? PAPER PERFECT. Every few years a newspaper story will report that players at a local bridge game were witness to a "perfect deal": that is, each player got all 13 cards of a suit. How many of these deals would you expect to occur anywhere in the world during this decade?

148. COMPUTERS

A computer buff called Hacker owns several computers. All but two of them are Apples, all but two of them are Commodores and all but two of them are IBMs. How many computers does our friend Hacker own?

149. THIRD OF THE PLANET

How far from the centre of the Earth would you have to be to see one-third of the planet's surface?

150. CHECKERS

Take 16 draughts—8 black and 8 white—and arrange them as shown below, in a 4 x 4 square with the colours alternating in checkerboard fashion. If you don't have draughts, coins will do, with the "head" and "tail" sides substituting for the two different colours.

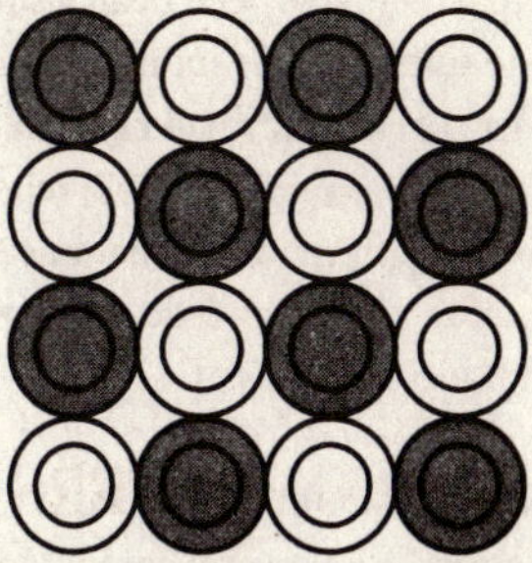

The problem is to rearrange the draughts within a 4 x 4 square so that each column is just one colour—either all black or all white. You could easily solve the problem if you were allowed to touch 8 draughts in the square and, with a little figuring, you may find ways to do it by touching only 6. The problem can be solved, however, by touching only 2 draughts in the whole array. How would you do it?

151. THE HANDICAP RACE

Mel and Sid race each other in a 100-yard dash. Mel wins by 10 yards. They decide to race again, but this time, to make things fairer, Mel begins 10 yards behind the starting line. Assuming they both run with the same constant speed as before, who wins this time, Mel or Sid? Or is it a draw?

152. . . . 9, 10

Where would you place 9 and 10 to keep the sequence going?

1	2				6		
		3	4	5		7	8

153. THE SOUTH POLE

Base to explorer at the South Pole: "What's the temperature?" "Minus 40 degrees," said the explorer. "Is that Centigrade or Fahrenheit?" asked base. "Put down Fahrenheit," said the explorer. "I don't expect it will matter.' Why did he say that?

154. GUINNESS OR STOUT

Two strangers enter a pub. The barman asks them what they would like.

First man says, "I'll have a bottle of stout," and puts 50 pence down on the counter.

Barman: "Guinness at 50 pence, or Jubilee at 45 pence?"

First man: "Jubilee."

Second man says, "I'll have a bottle of stout," and puts 50 pence on the counter. Without asking him, the barman gives him Guinness.

How did the barman know what the second man was drinking?

155. BONUS PAYMENTS

A company offered its 350 employees a bonus of £10 to each male and £8.15 to each female. All the females accepted, but a certain percentage of the males refused to accept. The total bonus paid was not dependent upon the number of men employed. What was the total amount paid to the women?

156. THE TILED FLOOR

A 2½-inch-square card is thrown at random on to a tiled floor (see figure below). What are the odds against its falling and not touching a line? You should assume that the pattern repeats over a large area.

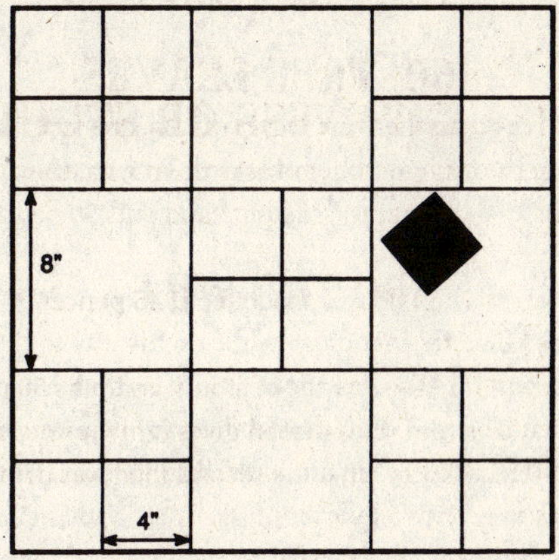

157. A SHUFFLED DECK

Prove that if the top 26 cards of an ordinary shuffled deck contain more red cards than there are black cards in the bottom 26, then there are in the deck at least 3 consecutive cards of the same colour.

158. A PECULIAR NUMBER

If a certain number is reduced by 7 and the remainder is multiplied by 7, the result is the same as when the number is reduced by 11 and the remainder is multiplied by 11. Find the number.

159. ANTIFREEZE

A 21-quart capacity car radiator is filled with an 18 percent alcohol solution. How many quarts must be drained and then replaced by a 90 percent alcohol solution for the resulting solution to contain 42 percent alcohol?

160. TREE LEAVES

If there are more trees than there are leaves on any one tree, then there exist at least two trees with the same number of leaves. True or false?

161. THE WILL

Daniel Greene was killed in a car crash while on his way to the maternity hospital where his wife, Sheila, was about to give birth. He had recently made a new will, in which he stated that, should the baby be a boy, his estate was to be divided two-thirds to his son and one-third to Sheila; if the baby were a girl, then she was to receive a quarter of the estate and Sheila the other three-quarters. In the event Sheila gave birth to twins—a boy and a girl. How best should Daniel's estate be divided so as to carry out his intention?

162. WATERED-DOWN WINE

Imagine you have two large jugs. One contains 10 litres of water and the other 10 litres of wine. One litre of wine is removed from the wine jug, poured into the water jug and mixed thoroughly. Then a litre of the mixture from the water jug is removed and poured into the wine jug.

Is there now more or less water in the wine jug than there is wine in the water jug?

163. A LOGIC RIDDLE

In olden days, the student of logic was given this problem: If half of 5 were 3, what would one-third of 10 be?

164. A MATTER OF HEALTH

If 70 percent of the population have defective eyesight, 75 percent are hard of hearing, 80 percent have sinus trouble and 85 percent suffer from allergies, what percentage (at a minimum) suffer from all four ailments?

165. TRAMLINES

A man is walking down a street along which runs a tramline. He notices that, for every 40 trams which pass him travelling in the same direction as him, 60 pass in the opposite direction. If the man's walking speed is 3 miles per hour, what is the average speed of the trams?

166. PASSING TRAINS

A man and a woman are walking along a railway track. A train passes the man in 10 seconds. Twenty minutes later, it reaches the woman. It passes her in 9 seconds. How long after the train leaves the woman will the man and woman meet if all speeds are constant?

167. THE FLY AND THE RECORD

A fly is walking around the groove of a 33 r.p.m. record. The record is lying flat on the floor, and when looked at from above, the fly appears to be travelling clockwise. If it carries on in this way, will it eventually arrive at the edge of the record or the centre?

168. MOVE ONE COIN

Ten coins are arranged as shown above. Can you move just one coin to another position so that, when added up either horizontally or vertically, two rows of 6 coins each will be formed? (It's best to try to find the solution using real coins.)

169. THE UNBALANCED COIN

You have a coin that you have reason to suspect is unbalanced; that is, it is biased towards heads or tails, and a long series of tosses won't come out 50-50. How can this coin be used to generate a series of random binary digits—ones and zeros?

170. BICYCLE EXPERIMENT

A rope is tied to a bicycle pedal that is stationary at the bottom of its arc (see above). If someone pulls back on the rope while another person holds the seat lightly to keep the bicycle balanced, will the bicycle move forward, backward, or not at all?

171. A PIECE OF STRING

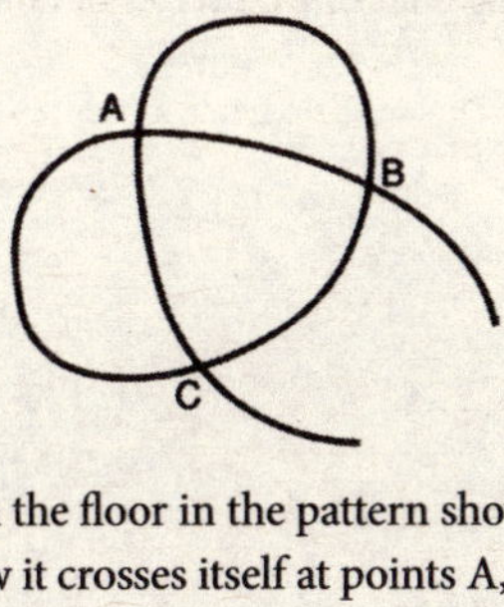

A piece of string, lying on the floor in the pattern shown above, is too far away for an observer to see how it crosses itself at points A, B and C. What is the probability that the string produces a knot if the ends are pulled apart?

172. THE ISLAND AND THE TREES

The figure below shows a deep circular lake, 300 yards in diameter, with a small island at the centre. The two black spots are trees.

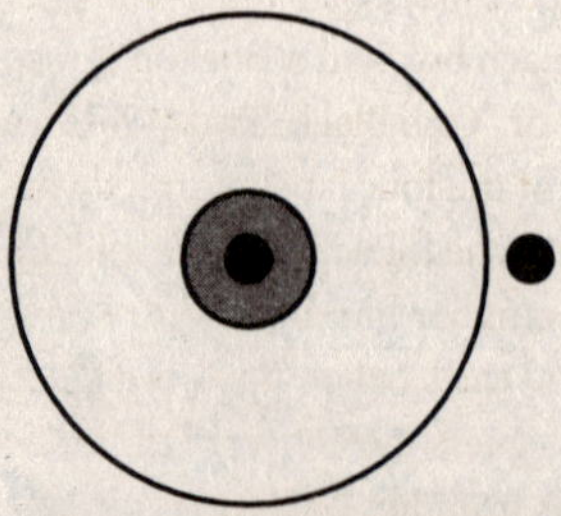

A girl who cannot swim has a rope a few yards longer than 300 yards. How does she use it as a means of getting to the island?

173. A BOY, A GIRL AND A DOG

A boy, a girl and a dog start at the same spot on a straight road. The boy walks forward at 4 miles per hour; the girl walks forward at 3 miles per hour. Meanwhile, the dog trots back and forth between them at 10 miles per hour. Assuming that each reversal of direction of the dog is instantaneous, where is it and which way is it facing after one hour?

174. BOXES AND BALLS

Four blindfolded girls were each given an identical box, containing different coloured balls. One contained 3 black balls; one contained 2 black balls and 1 white ball; one contained 1 black ball and 2 white balls; and the fourth contained 3 white balls. Each box had a label on it reading "Three Black" or "Two Black, One White" or "One Black, Two White" or "Three White." The girls were told that none of the four labels correctly described the contents of the box to which it was attached. Each girl was told, in turn, to draw 2 balls from her box, at which point her blindfold was removed so that she could see the 2 balls in her hand and the label on the box assigned to her. She was then given the task of trying to guess the colour of the ball remaining in her box.

As each girl drew balls from her box, their colours were announced for all the girls to hear; but the girls could not see the labels on any box other than their own.

The first girl, having drawn 2 black balls, announced: "I know the colour of the third ball." The second girl drew one white and one black ball, and similarly stated: "I know the colour of the third ball." The third girl withdrew two white balls, looked at her label, and said: "I can't tell what the colour of the third ball is." Finally, the fourth girl declared: "I don't need to remove my blindfold or any balls from my box, and yet I know the colour of all three. What's more, I know the colour of the third ball in each of your boxes as well."

The first three girls were amazed by the fourth girl's assertion and immediately challenged her. She proceeded to identify the contents of each box correctly. How?

175. TWO TRAINS

If it takes twice as long for a passenger train to pass a freight train after it first overtakes it as it takes for the two trains to pass each other when going in opposite directions, how many times faster than the freight train is the passenger train travelling?

176. MISSING ELEVATION

From the front elevation and the plan below, can you find the side elevation and describe the object?

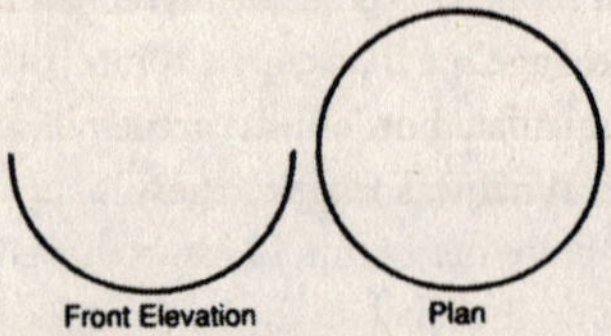

177. AVOIDING THE TRAIN

A man was walking down a railway track when he saw an express train speeding towards him. To avoid it he jumped off the track, but before he jumped he ran 10 feet towards the train. Why?

178. BOWL AND PAN

My mother has a bowl that holds a little more than a litre, and a flat rectangular, straight-sided pan that holds exactly a litre. The figure below shows its proportions.

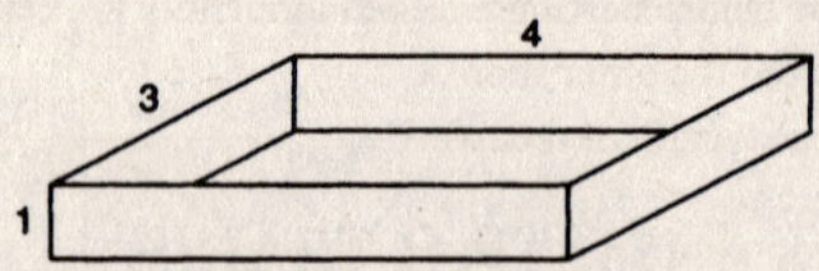

She wants to put exactly one-third of a litre of water into the bowl, but has no other means of measuring anything. She has a supply of water and an ordinary kitchen table with an exactly level surface. How does she do it?

179. JASMIN'S AGE

When Jasmin went to the polling station to vote, the clerk asked her age.

She told him, "Eighteen."

He looked at her, surprised, and said, "Are you sure that's right?"

Jasmin laughed and replied, "No, I gave myself the benefit of a year less than a quarter of my real age."

The clerk couldn't calculate how old she actually was, though he did allow her to register her vote. What was Jasmin's age?

180. A BALL OF WIRE

A wire of $\frac{1}{100}$ of an inch diameter is tightly wound into a ball with a diameter of 24 inches. It is assumed that the wire is bound so solidly that there is no air gap in the ball. What is the length of the wire?

181. FERRY BOATS

Two ferry boats start moving at the same instant from opposite sides of the Hudson River, one boat going from New York to Jersey City, and the other from Jersey City to New York. One boat is faster than the other, so they meet at a point 720 yards from the nearest shore.

After arriving at their destinations, each boat remains for 10 minutes to change passengers before starting on the return trip. The boats meet again at a point 400 yards from the other shore.

What is the exact width of the river?

182. JOHN AND THE CHICKEN

John was attempting to steal a chicken. When he first saw the bird, he was standing 250 yards due south of it. Both began running at the same time and ran with uniform speeds. The chicken ran due east. Instead of running northeast on a straight line, John ran so that at every instant he was running directly towards the chicken.

Assuming that John ran 1⅓ times faster than the chicken, how far did the chicken run before it was caught?

183. THE PRISONER'S CHOICE

A prisoner was about to be executed but was promised his freedom if he drew a silver ball from one of two identical urns. He was allowed to distribute 50 silver and 50 gold balls between the two urns any way he liked. The urns were then going to be shuffled around out of his sight and he was to pick one urn and draw one ball at random from that urn.

How did the prisoner maximize his chances of success? If he had put equal numbers of silver and gold balls into one of the urns, the other urn would also contain equal numbers of silver and gold balls, and thus the probability of his drawing a silver would have been 1 in 2. Can you improve these chances, and if so, how?

184. COUNTERS IN A CUP

I hesitated over whether to include this puzzle, as it straddles the fence between a trick question and a legitimate puzzle. However, the solution is especially neat.

How can 10 counters be distributed between 3 cups (see above) so that each cup contains an odd number of counters?

185. SPEED OF ANT

A train is approaching Kings Cross Station at 114 centmetres per second. A passenger in one carriage is walking forward at 36 cm per second relative to the seats. He is eating a 30cm hot dog, which is entering his mouth at the rate of 2cm per second. An ant on the hot dog is running away from the passenger's mouth at 1cm per second. How fast is the ant approaching Kings Cross?

186. WAYNE AND SHIRLEY

Wayne and Shirley have agreed that they would like to have a family of 4 children, but they would prefer not to have them all the same sex. Is it more likely that they will have 3 of one sex and 1 of the other or 2 of each? (Assume that each birth has an equal chance of being a boy or a girl, which, in the real world, is not statistically quite the case.)

187. WORD SERIES

What is the next word in the following series: *aid, nature, world, estate, column, sense* . . . ?

Is it (a) *water*, (b) *music*, (c) *welcome*, or (d) *heaven*?

188. SHOOTING MATCH

Two sharpshooters, Bill and Ben, had a contest to see which of them was the better shot. In their first session, each fired 50 rounds and hit the target 25 times. Later, they had a second session, and this time Bill hit the target 3 times in 34 shots, and Ben missed 25 shots in a row before giving up. Since Bill's record in the second session was better than Ben's, Bill argued that his record for the two sessions combined was better than Ben's. Was he right?

189. LETHARGIC LLAMAS

A zoo keeper houses 9 llamas all together in a large square cage.

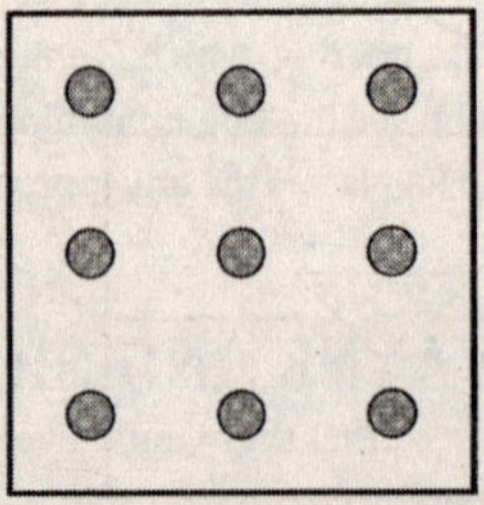

Strangely, all these llamas are very lethargic and remain in the positions shown in the figure above at all times. Can you give each its own private cage by building just 2 more square enclosures?

190. TORPID TAPIRS

The same zoo also has 10 torpid tapirs which are constantly positioned in a circular pen as shown below.

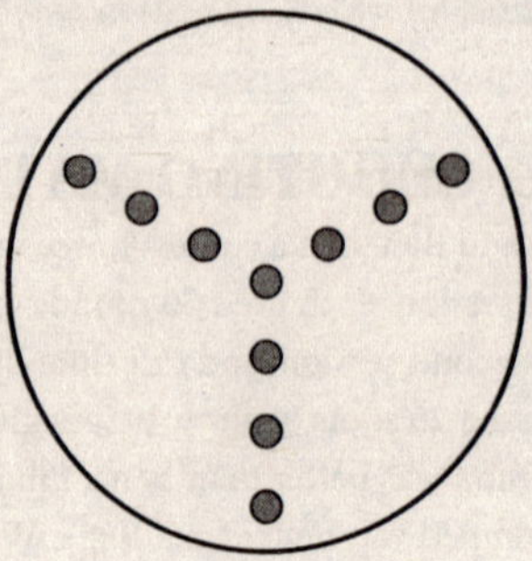

Give each tapir its own private compartment by drawing only 3 additional circular enclosures.

191. WOODEN BLOCK

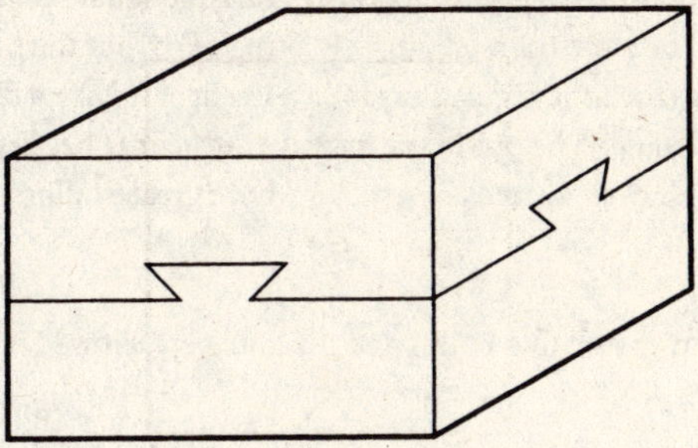

The wooden block shown above has been cut into two pieces and then reassembled. The pattern on the two hidden sides is the same as that on the two visible sides. How was this done?

192. WORD AFFINITY

All but one of the following have something in common. What is it, and which is the odd one out?

SOCK SICK BRICK BUS POCKET
FIELD LINE TIGHT FORCE LIFT

193. GUN PROBLEM

I have a gun I use for clay-pigeon shooting. This gun is 1.4 metres long. One day I wanted to take the train to join a shooting party, but the ticket clerk told me that it was against the regulations for a passenger to take a firearm into the carriage, and it couldn't be put in the baggage area either because the baggage handler wasn't allowed to take any articles whose greatest dimension exceeded 1 metre.

What did I do to ensure that both I and my gun were allowed on the train?

194. COUNTER COLOURS

A bag contains one counter, which may be either black or white. A second counter, which is definitely white, is put into the bag. The bag is shaken and one counter taken out, which proves to be white. What is the probability of the next counter coming out of the bag also being white?

195. BANK ACCOUNT

A bank customer had £100 in his account. He then made 6 withdrawals, totaling £100. He kept a record of these withdrawals, and the balance remaining in the account, as follows:

Withdrawals	Balance left
£50	£50
25	25
10	15
8	7
5	2
2	0
£100	£99

When he added up the columns as above, he assumed that he must owe £1 to the bank. Was he right?

196. HAT IN THE RIVER

A man wearing a straw hat was fishing from a rowing boat in a river that flowed at a speed of 3 miles per hour. The boat drifted down the river at the same rate.

Just as the man started to row upstream, the wind blew his hat off his head and into the water beside the boat. However, he didn't notice that his hat was gone until he had rowed 5 miles upstream, at which point he immediately started rowing back downstream to retrieve his hat.

The man's rowing speed in still water is a constant 5 miles per hour. However, when rowing upstream his speed relative to the shore would be only 2 miles per hour, given the rate of flow of the river. Rowing downstream, his speed relative to the shore would be 8 miles per hour for the same reason.

If the man lost his hat at 2 o'clock in the afternoon, what was the time when he retrieved it?

197. TOSSING PENNIES

Jill offered Jack the following bet: she said she would toss 3 coins in the air, and if they fell all heads or all tails she would give him £1. If they fell any other way, he had to give her 50p. Should Jack accept?

198. THE KINGS

Six playing cards are lying face down on the table. Two, and only two, of them are Kings, but you don't know which. You pick two cards at random and turn them face up. Which is more likely:

That there will be at least one King among the two cards; or

That there will be no King among the two cards?

199. TRAFFIC LIGHTS

The main street in our town has a linked traffic system consisting of 6 consecutive sections, each a multiple of ⅛ of a mile in length, and each terminating in a traffic light. These traffic lights have a 26-second cycle, which can be considered as 13 seconds on red and 13 seconds on green. The lights are synchronized so that a vehicle traveling at 30 miles per hour will pass each light at the same point in its cycle.

My brother, Albert, has studied the system and reckons he can drive faster than 30 miles per hour and still get through the entire system without crossing a red light. Recently, he set up an experiment with the help of two friends, Robert and Hubert. All three entered the first section simultaneously, Albert traveling at 30, Hubert at 50 and Robert at 75 miles per hour, with the first traffic light turning green 3 seconds later.

Robert got through the whole system in less than 2 minutes without being stopped. However, he thought he had been lucky, as he arrived at the last light just as it changed to red. Hubert ran out of petrol after the third light, and in any case would have been stopped at the second light had he not lost 10 seconds due to a delay in the second section.

What were the lengths of each of the 6 sections?

200. THE FEAST DAY

In a remote village in the Himalayas, a Feast Day is declared whenever the bells of the temple and the monastery ring at exactly the same time. The temple bell rings at regular intervals of a whole number of minutes. The monastery bell also rings at regular intervals, but of a different whole number of minutes. Today, the bells are due to ring together at 12 noon.

Between Feast Days, the bells of the temple and monastery ring alternately, and although they only coincide on Feast Days, they do occur as little as a minute apart on some of the other days.

The last time the bells coincided was at 12 noon a prime number of days ago. How many days ago was that?

201. THE CLOCK-MENDER

I have two clocks which, when fully wound, will run for nearly 8 days before stopping. Both of these clocks were keeping different times, and each was wrong by an exact number of minutes per day, though less than 1 hour in each case.

I took my clocks to be fixed. The local clock-mender works from 9:30 a.m. to 5:00 p.m., Mondays to Fridays. He immediately wound both clocks fully and set them to the right time—a whole number of minutes after the hour—then put them on a shelf for observation.

The following Monday, as he went to take down the clocks to start work on them, they both started to strike 8 o'clock simultaneously. This was some hours and minutes past the correct time. What day and exact time was it when the clock-mender set them originally?

202. THE BRIDGE

A-town and B-town are two villages connected by a bridge spanning a river. At the end of a war, the occupying forces installed a sentry in the middle of the bridge to prevent the inhabitants of A-town and B-town from visiting each other. All means of transport having been requisitioned, the only access from village to village is by foot over the bridge, which would take 10 minutes. The sentry is under strict orders to come out of his bunker every 5 minutes, and send anyone trying to cross back to his own village, if necessary by force of arms. Michael in A-town is desperate to visit his girlfriend in B-town. Is there a way?

203. THE COOKIE JAR

An old nursery rhyme starts: "Who stole the cookie from the cookie jar ..." Let us find out from the following statements, of which only one is true:

Ann: Harry stole the cookie from the cookie jar.
Harry: Fred stole the cookie from the cookie jar.
Lisa: Who me?—can't be.
Fred: Harry is lying when he says that I stole the cookie.

204. CROSSING THE DESERT

A small aeroplane carrying 3 men has to make an emergency landing in the middle of the desert. The men decide that their best chance for survival is for each of them to set out across the desert in a different direction, in the hope that one of them will be able to reach civilization and get help for the others. Their supplies include 5 full bottles of water, 5 half-full, and 5 empty bottles.

Since water-carrying capacity is important should a man reach an oasis, they wish to divide both the water supply and the number of bottles equally among themselves. How can they achieve this?

205. PANAMA CANAL

A ship entered the Panama Canal at its west end, passed through the canal, and left at its east end. However, immediately after it left the canal, it entered the Pacific Ocean. If the ship did not double back or sail backwards, how could this be?

206. THE SHORT CUT

John was trying to take a short cut through a very narrow tunnel when he heard the whistle of an approaching train behind him. Having reached three-eighths of the length of the tunnel, he could have turned back and cleared the entrance of the tunnel running at 10 miles per hour just as the train entered. Alternatively, if he kept running forward, the train would reach him the moment he would jump clear of the tracks. At what speed was the train moving?

207 RED, WHITE AND BLUE

This is a famous paradox which has caused a great deal of argument and disbelief from many who cannot accept the correct answer.

Four balls are placed in a hat. One is white, one is blue and the other two are red. The bag is shaken and someone draws two balls from the hat. He looks at the two balls and announces that at least one of them is red.

What are the chances that the other ball he has drawn out is also red?

208. COMMON FACTOR

What do the following words have in common?

DEFT FIRST CALMNESS CANOPY
LAUGHING STUPID HIJACK.

209. WORD GROUPS

Which word from Group 2 belongs with those in Group 1?

Group 1:	BAG	STORM	BANK	BAR
Group 2:	MOON	FLOOR	STORE	DUNE

210. TWO WINS

Bill is a keen chess player and often plays against his parents. He wins and loses against both parents, but his mother is a better player than his father.

His parents offer to double his allowance if he can win two games in a row out of three, with his parents alternating as opponents. Which parent should he play first to maximize his chances of winning two in a row?

211. FIND X

Solve the following equation for x:

$$\sqrt{x+\sqrt{x+\sqrt{x}}}\ \ldots = 2$$

212. POCKETFUL OF COINS

Freddy has 10 pockets and 44 coins. He wants to distribute the change among his pockets so that each pocket contains a different number of coins. Can he do this?

213. SIX-GALLON HAT

You bought a ten-gallon hat as a souvenir of a visit to Texas; only when you got home did you discover that the label states it to be only a six-gallon hat. By now, you were skeptical that it was even that big, and you decided to test it by trying to fill it with 6 gallons of water. The only containers you had to hand were those below. Using them, how were you able to pour 6 gallons into the hat?

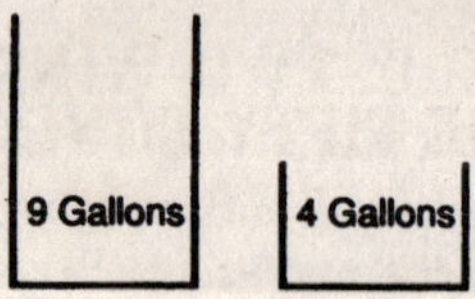

214. A FLOCK OF GEESE

Two brothers, Guy and George, inherited a flock of geese. They sold the entire flock, receiving for each goose the same number of pounds as there were geese in the flock. The money was given to them in £10 notes except the odd amount, less than £10, which was paid in change. They divided the notes by dealing them out alternately, though Guy complained that this was not fair because George received both the first and last notes, thus getting £10 more. To even things up, George gave Guy all the change, but Guy argued he was still worse off. George agreed to give Guy a cheque for the difference. What was the value of the cheque?

215. THREE POINTS ON A HEMISPHERE

Three points are selected at random on a sphere's surface. What is the probability that they all lie in the same hemisphere? Assume that the great circle, bordering a hemisphere, is part of the hemisphere.

216. DEAL A BRIDGE HAND

A man had dealt about half the cards for a bridge game when he was interrupted by a telephone call. When he returned, no one could remember who had been dealt the last card. Without knowing the number of cards in any of the 4 partly dealt hands, or the number of cards left in the undealt part of the pack, how could the deal be completed so that everyone received the cards they would have received had the deal not been interrupted?

217. THE FIFTY POND NOTE

The manager of the local bank found a £50 note lying in the gutter; he picked it up and made a note of its serial number. Later that day his wife mentioned that they owed the butcher £50, so the banker used the note he'd found to settle up with the butcher. The butcher used it to pay a farmer; the farmer in turn used it to pay his feedstock supplier; and the feedstock supplier used it to pay his laundry bill. The laundryman used it to pay off his £50 overdraft at the local bank. The banker recognized the note as being the one he had found in the gutter, but also noticed, on closer examination, that it was a fake. By now, it had been used to settle £250 worth of debts.

What was lost as a result of this series of transactions, and by whom?

218. THE BICYCLE RACE

Two cyclists are racing around a circular track. Pierre can ride once around the track in 6 minutes, Louis takes 4 minutes. How many minutes will it take for Louis to lap Pierre?

219. THE NORTH POLE

A man goes to the North Pole. The points of the compass are, of course:

N
W E
S

He reaches the Pole and, having passed over it, turns about to look North. East is now on his left-hand side, and West on his right-hand side, so the points of the compass appear to be:

N
E W
S

Is this correct? If not, what is the explanation?

220. CARD GAMES

Jack and Jill are playing cards for a stake of £1 a game. At the end of the evening, Jack has won 3 games and Jill has won £3. How many games did they play?

221. LONG-PLAYING RECORD

The diameter of a vinyl long-playing record is 12 inches. The unused part in the centre has a diameter of 4 inches and there is a smooth outer edge 1 inch wide around the recording. If there are 91 turns of the groove to the inch, how far does the needle move during the actual playing of one side of the record?

222. WHICH GAMES?

I have three friends. Two play football, two play tennis and two play golf. The one who does not play golf does not play tennis, and the one who does not play tennis does not play football. Which games does each friend play?

223. WHAT DAY IS IT?

When the day after tomorrow will be yesterday, today will be as far from Sunday as today was from Sunday when the day before yesterday is tomorrow. What day is it today?

224. CASH BAGS

A man went into a bank with exactly £1,000 in pound coins. He gave them to a cashier and asked the cashier to put the money into 10 bags in such a way that if he later needed any amount of coins up to £1,000, he could lay his hands on that amount without needing to open any of the bags. How did the cashier achieve this?

225. GARAGE SPACE

A haulage contractor did not have room in his garage for 8 of his trucks. He therefore increased the size of his garage by 50 percent, which gave him room for 8 more trucks than he owned altogether. How many trucks did he own?

226. BAG OF CHOCOLATES

Three girls agreed to share out a bag of chocolates in proportion to their ages. The sum of their ages was 17½ years, and the bag contained 770 chocolates. For every 4 chocolates Joan took, Jane took 3; for every 6 Joan took, Jill took 7. How many chocolates did each girl take, and what are their respective ages?

227. LOST

I am travelling in a strange country. I have no map. I come to a crossroads where the signpost has been knocked down. How can I find my way without asking anyone for directions?

228 PROBLEM AGE

The day before yesterday, Peter was 17. Next year he will be 20. How do you explain this?

229. HEX SIGN

The hex sign above is made up entirely of circles 1 centimetre in radius. Can you calculate the area of each of the shaded petal-shaped areas?

230. SQUARES FROM A SQUARE

Using only a straight-edge, construct 5 smaller squares, the areas of which will total that of the larger square.

231. THE GOAT

A man in Kansas pays rent to a local farmer who allows him to graze his pet goat on his (the farmer's) field. When on the field, the goat is tethered to a post by a 21-foot rope, so that the area on which it grazes is a circle with a radius of 21 feet. The farmer has decided to build a shed on the field, 14 feet by 7 feet, using the post as one of the corner posts of the shed (see below).

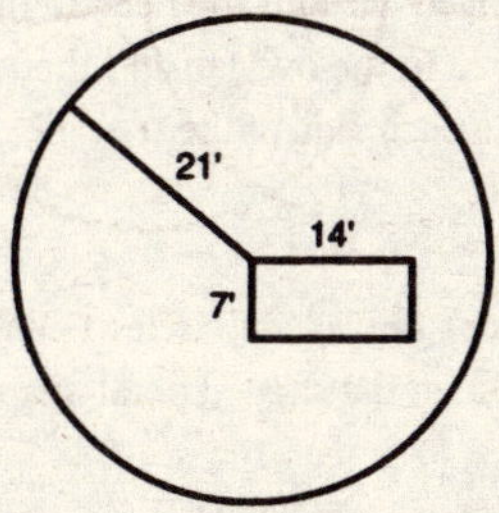

If the farmer has been charging the goat's owner $100 per annum, by how much should the rent be reduced to reflect the grazing area lost?

232. OVERLAPPING CIRCLES

In the figure below, 3 equal circles have been drawn so that each one passes through the centres of the other two. Is the area of overlap, shown shaded in the diagram, more or less than a quarter of the area of a circle?

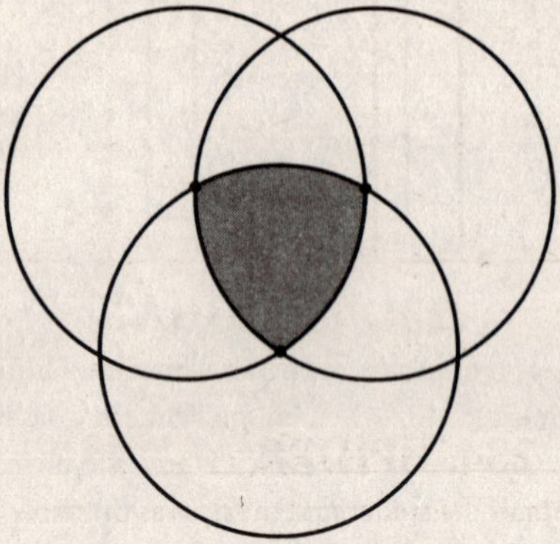

This problem can be solved without the need to find the area of the equilateral triangle inscribed in the overlap and then adding the areas of the 3 segments of circles on each side of the triangle. In fact, no geometrical formulae are required at all.

233. SIDEWAYS

The figure below shows a structure viewed from the front and from above. What does it look like from the side?

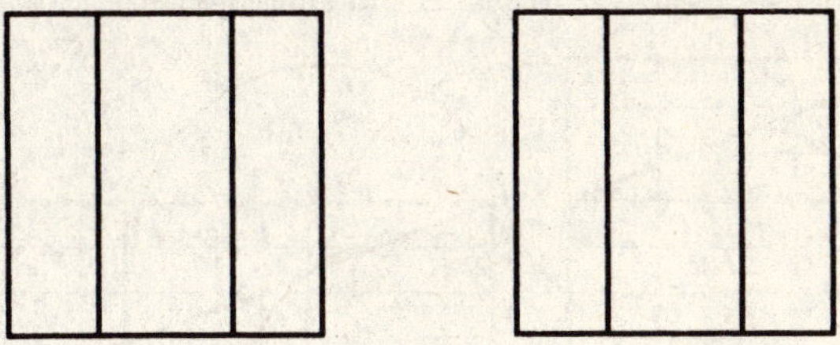

234. SPIDER AND FLY

The geodesic problem of the spider and the fly was probably Dudeney's most famous puzzle. It was first published in 1903, and aroused widespread public interest in 1905 when it appeared in the London *Daily Mail.*

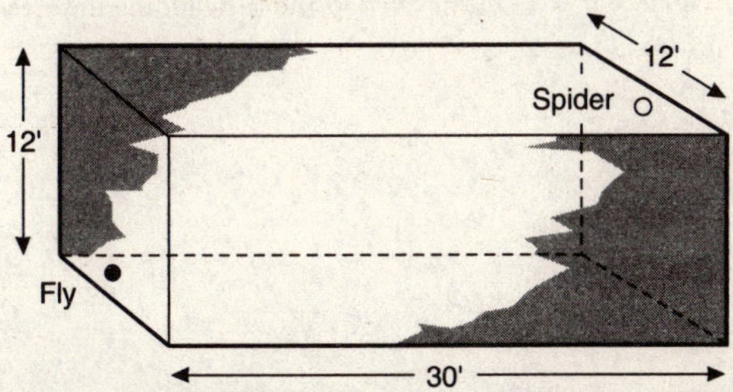

A rectangular room is 30 feet long, 12 feet wide and 12 feet high, as shown above. The spider is sitting 1 foot down from the ceiling at the center of one of the end walls. The fly is 1 foot above the floor at the center of the opposite end wall, and being petrified with fear is unable to move. What is the length of the shortest route the spider can take to get to the fly?

235. THE VANISHING SQUARE

Design a square as shown in figure A, with an area of 64 units. Cut the board along the lines indicated and rearrange as shown in figure B, which yields a rectangle with an area of 65 units.

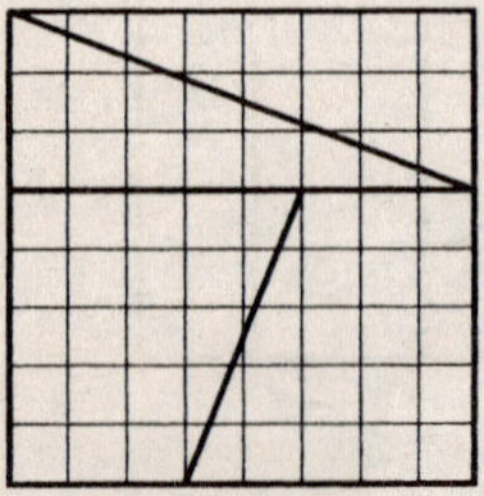

A Area = 8 x 8 = 64

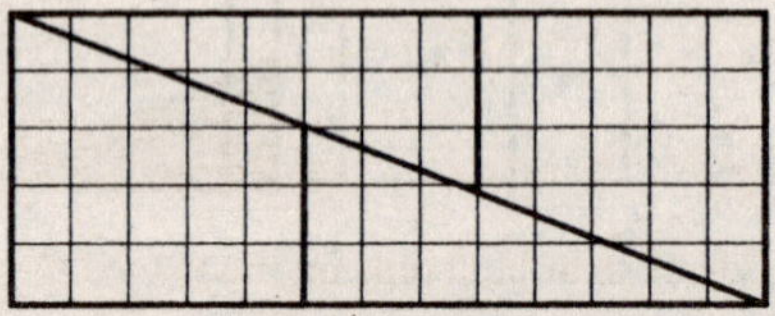

B Area = 5 x 13 = 65

The gain of one square can be explained by a long, thin, diamond-shaped gap along the diagonal of the 5 x 13 rectangle. This is hardly noticeable to the naked eye.

The story goes that a similar optical illusion was used by clever forgers to make 15 £20 notes out of 14 notes. How was this done?

236. THE AVENUE

The local residents' association has been complaining about the plans for a new housing estate in the town. The proposed site, as shown below, is a perfect square, each side being ¾ of a mile.

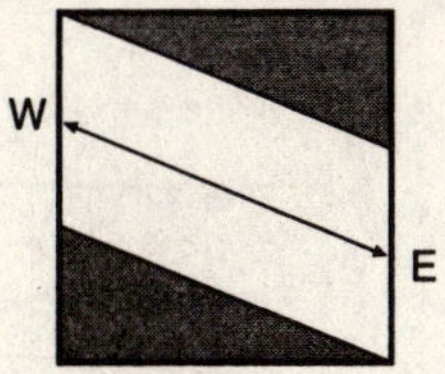

Houses are to be built only on the shaded areas, that is, the two identical triangular areas. The space in between, down the centre of which an avenue runs from west to east, is to be occupied by a communal garden.

It is the devotion of so much space to this garden—it occupies $^{7}/_{12}$ of the total area of the estate—that has provoked adverse criticism. What is the length of the central avenue?

SOLUTIONS

1. The Heir

The test was a blood test. The elder remembered that the true prince was a haemophiliac.

2. Death in the Car

The victim was in a convertible. He was shot when the top was down.

3. A Soldier's Dream

The soldier had his dream while on guard duty.

4. The Judgment

The convicted killer was one of Siamese twins.

5. The Jilted Bride

No. She had simply jammed the clapper with packed snow, which melted during the course of the ceremony.

6. Crafty Cabby

The woman realized the cabby could hear because he drove her to her requested destination.

7. The Sharpshooter

The sharpshooter's hat was hanging over the barrel of his gun.

8. Death In Squaw Valley

The clerk remembered having issued flight tickets to the banker, who had booked a return trip for himself and a one-way for his wife.

9. Burglars

Arthur is 10 months old.

10. Insomnia

Pete was being kept awake by Dave's snoring.

11. The North Pole

The odds are zero. In other words, the distance cannot be larger. For Eucla, or any other spot, to be 15,000 kilometres from the Pole it must be on the same parallel as Porto Allegre. But the circumference of the Earth at the Equator is near enough 40,000 kilometres and only slightly less (because of the flattening effect) around the Poles. Therefore the maximum distance between any two locations on the 30° parallel, via the South Pole, is approximately 10,000 kilometres.

12. The Long Division

10. Start at the end and work towards the beginning. Nine-tenths of 100 is 90. Eight-ninths of 90 is 80. Seven-eighths of 80 is 70. And so on until you come to one-half of 20.

13. Pool Resources

Jim has £5 and Andrew £7. There are two clues to the solution. The difference must be £2 to balance, and the original holdings must be odd numbers otherwise Andrew, having received £1, can never have twice Jim's amount.

Using an equation, let Jim's amount be *x* and Andrew's *y*.

Then: $2(x - 1) = (y + 1)$

and $(y - 1) = (x + 1)$

or $y = x + 2$

Therefore:

$$2(x - 1) = x + 3$$

$$2x - 2 = x + 3$$

$$x = 5$$

$$y = 7$$

14. The Parking Dodge No. 1

After the meeting Clive approached the first policeman he could find and told him in broken German:

"Officer, I have a terrible problem, can you help me? I don't know my way around Zurich. I have parked my car somewhere near the lake and for the last hour I have been searching frantically, but I cannot find it."

The Swiss police might be tough on parking offenders but they are also helpful to foreign tourists. Clive's car was found within 30 minutes and, needless to say, there was no question of a penalty.

15. The Parking Dodge No. 2

He removed a parking ticket from another car and stuck it on his. On leaving the theatre he replaced it, if the offending car was still there. If not he discarded it. Not strictly cricket, is it?

16. The Blip

The agent recorded a one and a half minute message on tape, then speeded it up two hundred times and transmitted it to Riyadh. The recipients slowed down the blip by the same factor.

They knew that it was their man who had sent the message because his speech pattern had been recorded on an oscilloscope which reduced it to a series of lines which are as positive an identification as a fingerprint. They also knew that he was transmitting as a free agent because they had agreed with him certain pre-arranged words or intonation to indicate if he were acting under duress.

17. A Wartime Mystery

When the KGB chief entered the conference room, Topolev recognized the civilian, Klaus Von Hasseldorf, aide-de-camp to the German ambassador Count Schulenberg. Topolev immediately realized that Hasseldorf was spying for the KGB. Topolev in turn was betraying his country to the Germans and in fact Hasseldorf had acted as his minder. Only a few days later on June 22nd 1941, at 4 a.m., Ribbentrop delivered a formal declaration of war to the Russian ambassador in Berlin.

18. The Black Forest

The man was a fighter pilot in the German air force. His plane had developed engine trouble and he had to bail out. His parachute got tangled up in the tree in such a way that the pilot was unable to free himself and after a few days he had died of exposure.

19. The Cabin in the Woods

The night before an explosion was heard and a fireball in the air noticed by several villagers, who reported it to the constabulary. It was assumed that the observation was caused by a plane crash and Hansel and Gretel were sent out to investigate. What they discovered in the woods was the cabin of an aeroplane.

20. The Sixpack

The answer is more complex than one would think. To start with, George would feel a reduction of the load he was carrying. His total weight (including remaining cans) would not diminish but the strain on his muscles would. After a short time George would lose weight through increased perspiration.

21. The Gamblers

Ian and Emma had booked a suite aboard a luxury cruise liner. On the fourth day there was an explosion in the engine room as a result of which the ship sank. Some passengers were saved though many passengers drowned, including Ian and Emma.

22. Spirit of St. Louis

Lindbergh was twice as safe with his single-engine plane.

The argument runs as follows:

Suppose the manufacturer has produced a batch of 100 engines of which one was faulty. The probability that this was Lindbergh's engine was 1%. Had he flown a twin-engine plane from the same batch the probability would have been 2%.

23. The Appointment

Gerry was broke and decided to hitchhike. He was unlucky in getting lifts and lost time waiting in Long Beach and Oceanside.

24. The Telephone Call

Father and child; or paternal uncle/aunt and nephew/niece.

25. Relations

Jill is Jean's mother; alternatively, Jean is the daughter of Jack's wife's brother or sister.

26. Sisters

They are two of a set of triplets or quadruplets, etc.

27. How Close?

Father.

28. The Painting

The man's own son.

29. Sons' Ages

There are only fourteen combinations of ages that satisfy the first clue, even allowing for two of the sons to be twins. (They can't all be triplets if their ages, in whole years, add up to 13.) The second man knows his own age, and yet the second clue doesn't give him the answer, so his age must be 36—the only product that occurs twice among the fourteen possible combinations.

The third clue indicates that there is only one oldest son, not two, ruling out the combination 6, 6, and 1, and leaving 9, 2 and 2 as the answer.

30. Father and Grandfather

Yes. It is perfectly possible for one's maternal grandfather to be younger than one's father.

31. Four Families

The reason we figured we might have to skip the game was that, thanks to the flu, fewer than 18 kids showed up at the park that Saturday.

There are only fourteen different combinations of numbers that add up to 17 or less and still allow each of our four families to have a different number of kids. Eleven of the fourteen possible combinations give you different totals if you multiply the numbers together, the other three all give you the same total: 120.

That's how many votes I told the wiseguy he was going to get on election day; that's why he had to ask his question about the Blacks.

The three combinations that give you 120 when the numbers are multiplied are: 8, 5, 3, 1; 6, 5, 4, 1; and 5, 4, 3, 2. So when the would-be mayor asked me "Do the Blacks have more than one child?" I must have answered "Yes," otherwise he wouldn't have been able to figure out how many kids each of our families had: 5,4, 3 and 2.

32. Husbands and Fathers

After their respective parents divorced, or their mothers died, Mary and Joan married each other's father. Alternatively, of course, their respective parents may never have been married in the first place.

33. How Many Children?

Four boys and three girls.

34. Boys and Girls

The traditional answer is as follows:

No, the sultan's plan would not work. Of the first children born to all the women, half would be boys and half girls. Only the latter half would be allowed to bear a second round of children, and, again, half of this round would be boys and half girls. Again, the mothers of the boys would drop out, leaving (on average) a quarter of the original number of mothers to have a third round of children, which again would be evenly split between boys and girls.

In any round of births, the ratio between boys and girls would never change and, therefore, in aggregate there will always be as many boys as girls.

The above solution is not entirely accurate. In fact, the sultan's law *may indirectly* result in more girls being born than boys or, for that matter, more boys being born than girls. This is not for the reason the sultan had in mind, but because of the way the law of averages operates.

The question assumes that the natural birth ratio between boys and girls is 50-50. But like all averages, the average only holds true over an infinite number of attempts (in this case, births). Over any finite number, the average is unlikely to hold precisely true, and the smaller the finite number the greater the likely deviation from the average. Thus, in the first round of births in the sultan's country, the incidence of boys and girls is unlikely to be exactly equal; how one-sided it is will depend on how many expectant mothers there are. If the first round of births produces more girls than boys, the sultan's law will have the effect of reducing the opportunity for the law of averages to "even out" the discrepancy; this evening-out opportunity is reduced progressively as every round of births further restricts the pool of mothers. The same is true if the first round of births produces more boys than girls.

35. Two Children

Since I have two children, at least one of which is a boy, there are three equally probable cases: Boy-Boy, Boy-Girl or Girl-Boy. In only one case are both children boys, so the probability that both are boys is 1-3.

My sister's situation is different. Knowing that the older child is a girl, there are only two equally probable cases: Girl-Girl or Girl-Boy. Therefore the probability that both children are girls is 1- 2.

36. Marital Problem

Jason and Dean were both clergymen. Dean married Jason to Denise, which explains why they share the same wedding anniversary. Jason married Jackie to a man whose name happens to be Peter. On another occasion, John married Dean to a girl called Paula.

37. Railways

Rails expand with rising temperature and, traditionally, gaps between rail sections have been considered an essential element of track design to accommodate this expansion and prevent buckling.

If the temperature of x feet of rails is raised by t degrees, then the length increases by an amount of $0.000006\,xt$.

However, since the 1950s, this conventional wisdom has undergone some rethinking. It is now accepted that rails can be welded together into lengths of up to half a mile and even longer, without a break, increasing stability by anchoring the rails more closely to the ties; and in laying rails at a time when the temperature is close to, or slightly in excess of, the mean temperature of the site, it has proven possible to reduce the effects of heat expansion significantly.

38. Rice and Salt

Rice is more hygroscopic than salt and therefore tends to keep the salt dry.

39. Coal and Lime

The lime solution covers the coal with a white film. If coal is stolen after loading and spraying, it is evident that the theft was committed en route and is easily discovered as the train passes stations on the way to its destination.

40. Sand on the Beach

Before you step on it, the sand is packed as tightly as it can be under natural conditions. Your weight disturbs the sand, making the grains less efficiently packed. The sand is forced to occupy more volume, and rises above the water level, becoming dry and white. The water rises more slowly, by capillary action, so it takes a few seconds or more before the sand gets wet and dark again.

41. Bridge Clearance

The child's solution was elementary. "Let some air out of your tires," she said, "until the truck is low enough to pass under the bridge."

42. A Flat Tyre

The man took one lug nut from each of the other three wheels, and attached the spare wheel. Each wheel was then held on by 3 nuts rather than 4, which was sufficient to keep the wheels on until the man reached the next town.

43. The Biology Exam

The student said, "Good, I didn't think so." He then jammed his test booklet into the middle of the stack and dashed out of the room. At least, so, proverbially, the story goes.

However, I can think of a sequel. The professor, a member of MENSA, refused to be outwitted by the smart-ass of a student. After marking the papers, he invited the students to collect their grades in person.

44. The Manhole

If, while being manoeuvered, a square manhole cover happened to be turned on its edge, so that it was presented diagonally to the manhole, it would fall through the manhole.

45. Wet Roof

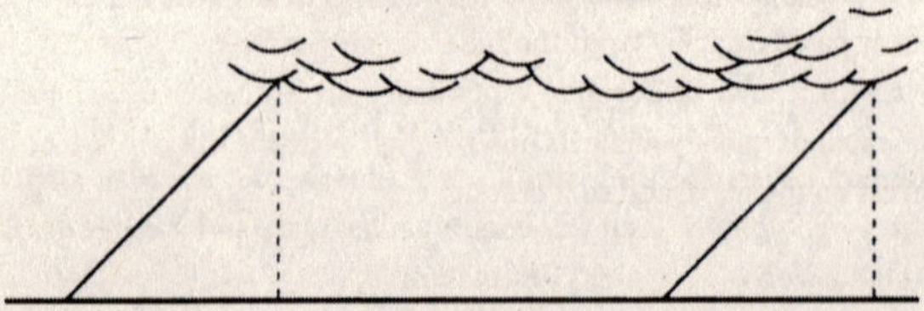

The figure above shows the rain from a 10-mile stretch of clouds falling at an angle of 45°. It wets the same extent of ground as it would if it fell vertically, but moved to the left. The point here is that the ground area is being compared with the cloud area, with which it is parallel, but in the case of the tilted roof described in the question, it was not. Thus, 10 miles of cloud wet 10 miles of ground, whereas 10 inches of cloud wet 14 inches of roof.

46. Inner Space

Down a mineshaft, the gravitational effect would be less because some of the Earth's mass is above you. That mass pulls you up, so it cancels the effect of some of the mass below your feet that pulls you down.

The point of this question is to show that gravity does not come from one source of attraction at the centre of the Earth, as many people suppose, but comes from the combined attraction of all the parts of the globe working together. Our idealized Earth of "uniform density" is fictional, of course, and in practice gravity would increase slightly as one got closer to the Earth's dense nickel-iron core. But as one descends into the core, the effect of gravity would be less and less, and at the Earth's centre it would be zero.

47. Weigh-in

The fluctuations result from the up-and-down movement of your blood's center of gravity as your heart goes through its pumping cycle. For a person weighing 165 lb, there is a fluctuation of about 1 ounce with every heartbeat.

48. The Rifle

Both bullets will hit the ground at the same time. Horizontal velocity does not affect downward acceleration.

49. Cracked Up

The thick drinking glass will break first. Glass is a poor conductor of heat. In the thin wine glass, heat passes quickly from the inner to the outer surface of the glass, and the glass expands with relative uniformity. When you pour hot water into the thick glass, its inner surface expands quickly while its outer surface remains the same size; this results in enormous stress on the glass, and so it cracks.

50. Roll-off

The ball will reach bottom first because it has less of its mass on the outside, which gives it less angular (turning) inertia. The ring rolls most slowly because, with its mass distributed away from the centre of rotation, it has more inertial resistance to turning. For similar reasons, a figure skater can spin faster when her arms are tucked in close to her body.

51. Mountain Time

A mechanical watch runs faster in the mountains. The principal reason is the low atmospheric pressure and air density at high altitudes; the balance wheel has less air to push around, so it oscillates a bit faster.

Some infinitesimal effects may be predicted from the theory of relativity and will operate on electronic watches as well as wind-up ones. Einstein's theory says that time moves more slowly as (a) gravity increases and (b) velocity increases. The lessened gravity in the mountains would make a watch run relatively faster. This effect would be counteracted very slightly by the fact that, in the mountains, you're further from the Earth's axis of rotation and therefore travelling through space at a slightly faster rate, which would slow time.

52. Launch Pads

Spacecraft are launched in the direction of the Earth's rotation, from west to east. To take advantage of the maximum "push" from the Earth, launch sites are located as close to the equator as possible.

53. Poles Apart

Antarctica is a continent, and land is a poor heat conserver, so Antarctica's ice doesn't really melt readily. The Arctic is over an ocean, which has a high heat capacity. It warms the surface, melting much of the Arctic's ice.

54. Hard Skate

It's harder to ice skate when the air temperature is very cold. We tend to think of ice as inherently slippery, but it isn't. When you skate, the ice beneath your skates' sharp runners melts temporarily, creating a thin lubricating film of water. When it is very cold, the ice does not melt readily; this makes the ice feel "sticky" and harder to skate on.

55. The Suspended Egg

First fill the glass half full of water and dissolve enough salt in it to make it dense enough for the *egg* to float on top. Then add more unsalted water to the top, filling to the brim.

56. Two Bars of Iron

Take either bar and push one end against the middle of the other bar, forming a T. If the magnetized bar is the top of the T, there is no pull on the other bar.

57. The Bird Cage

If the bird is in a completely airtight box, the weight of the box and the bird will be the same whether the bird is flying or perching. If the bird is flying, its weight is borne by the air pressure on its wings; but this pressure is then transmitted by the air to the floor of the box. If the bird is flying in an open cage, part of the increase in pressure on the air is transmitted to the floor of the cage, but part is transmitted to the atmosphere outside the cage. Hence the cage with the bird will be lighter if the bird is flying.

58. Exception to the Rule

Water expands below 3.98°C (39.164°F) down to 0°C (32°F).

Otherwise, ice would be heavier than water, with catastrophic consequences. For instance, lakes and oceans would freeze from the bottom up, destroying marine life as we know it.

59. Water Level Problem

The water level neither rises nor falls: it stays the same. The reason an ice cube floats is because its volume has expanded during crystallization. Its weight remains the same as the weight of the water that formed it. Since a floating body displaces its weight, when the ice cube has melted it will provide the same amount of water as the volume of water it displaced when it was frozen.

60. Boat in the Bath

The nuts, bolts and washers in Rupert's boat displace an amount of water equal to their weight. When they sink to the bottom of the bath, they displace an amount of water equal to their volume. Since each item weighs considerably more than the same volume of water, the water level in the bath goes down after the cargo is dumped.

61. Space Station

Zero gravity would prevail at all points inside a hollowed-out asteroid, so it would float permanently at the same location.

62. Bird on the Moon

The bird couldn't fly at all on the moon because there is no lunar air to support it.

63. The Goldfish

The scale registers an increase in weight equivalent to the amount of liquid displaced by the suspended goldfish.

64. Speed of Sound

The speed of sound remains at 740 miles per hour; it does not get an extra "push" by approaching you. The sound waves will be crowded closer together, however, resulting in a higher pitch, known as the Doppler effect.

65. Two Bridges

The smaller bridge is twice as strong. If a steel girder, B, is twice the size of girder A in every dimension, it will be twice as strong as girder A but it will weigh eight times as much. The double-sized bridge could be so weak that it would collapse under its own weight.

66. Two Sailboats

Neglecting their weight, big sails are just as strong as small ones. The reasoning of the previous problem doesn't apply in this case, because as the size of a sail grows the force of the wind against the sail grows at the same rate.

In practice, the weight of the sail has to be taken into account; similarly, since winds 20 metres up are liable to be fiercer than winds only 10 metres up, a larger sail will be made of stronger fabric than a small sail. The point of the question, in contrast to the previous one, is that the load on a sail (in the form of wind pressure) does not increase as the cube of the linear dimension, as the load does on a bridge (in the form of weight).

67. Aircraft Temperature

The pressurized cabin in an airliner keeps air compressed to sea-level pressures. At a high altitude, this would raise the cabin temperature to 55°C or higher if air-conditioners were not used to extract heat from the air.

68. Fan Power

Strange as it seems, the fan will propel the boat—backwards! The reason is that not all of the wind generated by the fan is caught by the sail. The forward action is not enough to counter the backward reaction, so the boat is propelled backwards.

69. Flags

The flags show a star shining between the horns of a crescent moon. Since this area is the unlit portion of the moon, any stars in that part of the sky would be hidden.

70. Where Are You?

Try to spin one of your coins on the floor of your room: the coin will refuse to spin. By conservation of angular momentum, a spinning object tries to maintain its position in space. Since the spinning station is continually changing your position in space, a coin that is spun will keep changing its orientation, to correct its angular momentum, and will topple and fall.

71. Bridge Towers

To compensate for the curvature of the Earth.

72. Drops and Bubbles

The bubbles would move towards each other. If water is removed from one spot in all space (bubble A), the gravitational balance surrounding it is upset, and the net effect on a nearby molecule of water is that it is drawn towards greater mass; that is outwards, away from the bubble. If there are two bubbles, the water between them acts as if it is repelled from both, and the bubbles would move towards each other.

73. Special Sphere

Since a 20-foot-diameter sphere of 300 lb would weigh less than an equal volume of air (about 330 lb at sea level and 32°F, given pressure of 0.081 lb per cubic foot with air density at 14.7 lb per square inch), the sphere would rise into the air. It would level off at several thousand feet and could remain there for years, riding the winds.

74. The Striking Clock

Four seconds—the time between the clapper striking the bell for the first peal and the second one is 2 seconds, and 2 seconds later it strikes for the third peal. Do not be confused by the lingering sound—I said strike!

75. Red or Green

Most people erroneously include No. 4 in their answer. But consider: No. 2 does not matter, since the question is concerned only with red cards. If No. 1 has a circle, the answer to the question is NO. Similarly, if No. 3 is red the answer is NO. If No. 1 is a square, No. 3 is green, and No. 4 is either red or green the answer is YES. Therefore the answer is: No. 1 and No. 3.

76. The River

5⅓ (5 minutes 20 seconds).

Speed downstream is ½ km per minute. Return speed is ¼ km per minute. Therefore the current makes ⅛ of a kilometre difference per minute.

Consequently, the boat speed is ⅜ of a kilometre per minute, which translates into 5⅓ minutes for the 2 kilometres in still water.

77. Changing the Odds

The boy picked a pebble out of the hat and, before they had a chance to examine it, dropped it, apparently accidentally, where it was lost among the pebbles on the ground. He then pointed out to the king that the colour of the dropped pebble could be ascertained by checking the colour of the one remaining in the hat.

78. Zeno's Paradox

Achilles would reach the tortoise at $1{,}111^{1}/_{9}$ metres. If the race track is shorter than this, the tortoise would win. If it were exactly this size, it would be a tie. Otherwise Achilles will pass the tortoise.

79. The Boy and the Girl

The boy has red hair, the girl black hair. There are four possible combinations: true-true, true-false, false-true, and false-false. It is not the first, since we are told that at least one statement is false. Nor is it the second or third because, in each case, if one lied, then the other could not have been telling the truth. Therefore it is the fourth; both lied.

80. Infinity and Limits

The increasing radii will in fact approach a limit that is about 12 times that of the original circle.

81. Hats In the Wind

The probability is zero. If 9 people have their own hats, then the tenth must too.

82. Handshakes

Even. If you were to ask everyone in the world how many hands he or she has shaken, the total would be even because each handshake would have been counted twice—once each by the two people who shook hands. A group of numbers whose sum is even cannot contain an odd number of odd numbers.

83. Move One

Move the vertical bar of the + sign to the other side of the equation so that it now reads:

VI–II = IV

There is a second solution:

VII–II = V

84. A Chiming Clock

An hour and a half—from 12:15 to 1:45. When you have heard the clock chime once 7 times, you need not wait for it to chime again, for the next cannot be anything but 2 o'clock.

85. Ring Around the Circle

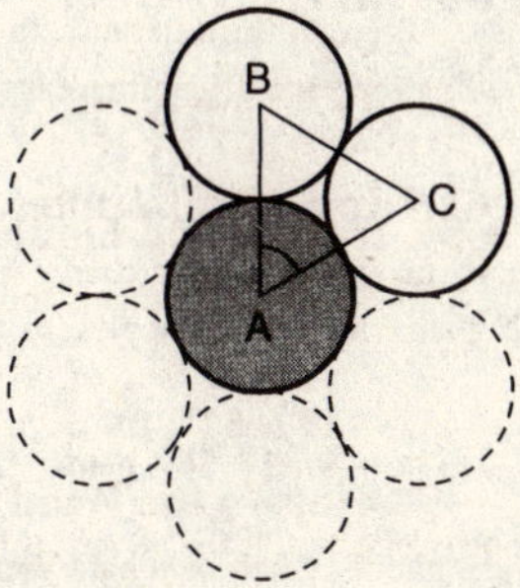

Exactly 6 circles will complete the ring. For the proof, inscribe the Δ ABC in the centre circle and two of the outer circles. The triangle is equilateral, since each side is equivalent to two radii. In equilateral triangles, each angle is 60°. Therefore Δ A is 60°, or one-sixth of a 360° circle.

86. A Unique Number

It is the only one that contains all the numerals in alphabetical order.

87. The Boss and His Chauffeur

For 50 minutes. He saved the chauffeur 10 minutes of travelling time each way and thus was picked up at 4:50 p.m., rather than the usual time.

88. Weather Report

The five temperatures were: 1,−1,2, −2, and 3.

89. Can You?

This statement was made by a salmon fisherman who was asked what he did with all the fish he caught.

90. Presidents

If the fifth president were not among those who died on that date, then the newspaper item would almost certainly have made the more impressive statement: "Three of the first four presidents died on the Fourth of July." Therefore, Professor Flugel was reasonably confident that the fifth president, James Monroe, died on that date.

91. Jim and George

They are standing back-to-back.

92. Two Sizes of Apples

This is a common trap in mathematical tests. The charge for the apples should be 33⅓ pence for large apples and 20 pence for smaller apples, so the average charge per apple should be:

$$(33\tfrac{1}{3} + 50)/2 = 26\tfrac{2}{3} \text{ pence}$$

and not 25 pence, which the boy collected. If the 60 apples had been sold for 26⅔ pence each, the boy would have received

$$60 \times 26\tfrac{2}{3} \text{ pence} = £16$$

The son was charging too little for the apples and the £1 went to the customers.

93. The Sequence

The solution is:

O T T F F S S E N ...

being the initial letters of One, Two, Three, Four, Five, Six, etc.

94. The Half-full Barrel

All they had to do was tilt the barrel on its bottom rim till the water was just about to pour out. If the barrel is exactly half full, the water level at the bottom of the barrel should just cover all the rim. That way half the barrel is full of water; the other half is air space. If the water amply covers the bottom rim, the barrel is more than half full; if the bottom is not fully covered, the barrel is less than half full.

95. The Marksman

The marksman who fires 5 shots in 5 seconds takes 1¼ seconds between shots, since there are 4 intervals between the first and last shots. The other marksman requires 10 seconds for 9 intervals, or $1^1/_9$ seconds between shots. Therefore, the second marksman will take less time to fire 12 shots—$12^2/_9$ seconds compared with 13¾ seconds.

96. The Square Table

Let's examine the problem from the point of view of any one of the women. Initially, since she is a woman, she reasons that her neighbours' hands would be raised regardless of whether the unseen individual was a man or a woman. But after further thought it occurs to her that if the person opposite was actually a man, he would have known immediately that the person sitting opposite him was a woman because his neighbours would have raised their hands only for that reason. Since the unseen person did not make this announcement, it could only be because she was a woman.

97. The Marbles

Only 2 marbles can be transferred out of the first bag. The contents of the 2 bags will then be one of the following:

	First bag			*Second bag*		
	Col. A	*Col. B*	*Col. C*	*Col. A*	*Col. B*	*Col. C*
1st possibility	*3*	*3*	*1*	*3**	*3**	*5*
2nd possibility	*3*	*2*	*2*	*3*	*4*	*4*

To assure at least 2 of each colour in the first bag, at least 7 marbles must be transferred back, because the first 6 might be the 3 colour A and the 3 colour B marbles represented by the starred 3s in the first possibility shown above. Therefore, there will be 4 marbles remaining in the second bag.

98. A Carbon Copy

He must start in the lower left corner.

99. Walking in Step

Whenever they step out together, it will always be on the left foot.

100. Razor Shortage

One's first thought is that the first shopper would take £3 and the second £5. But this is not correct.

The £8 was in payment for $\frac{8}{3}$ packs of razors. It follows then, that the equivalent of 8 full packs would be £24. So one pack is worth £3. Since we each ended up with $\frac{8}{3}$ packs, the first shopper, who had 3 packs to start with, gave me $\frac{1}{3}$ of a pack; the other $\frac{7}{3}$ were given by the other shopper. Therefore, £1 goes to the first shopper and £7 to the second.

101. Unusual Equations

(a) $5\overset{\downarrow}{4}5 + 5 = 550$

(b) $99 + \frac{9}{9} = 100$

(c) $.\frac{7}{7} \times .\frac{7}{7} = 100$

(This solution is somewhat flawed, as, strictly speaking, zeros should be used thus: *0.7.* Besides, the same principle can be applied to any number; n/0.n × n/0.n always equals 100!)

(d) $\frac{9+9}{.9}$

(Again, the divisor should read 0.9.)

102. The d'Alembert Paradox

No, his reasoning was incorrect. D'Alembert made the error of not carrying through his analysis far enough. The three cases are not equally likely, and the only way to obtain equally likely cases is, in the third case, to toss the coin again even when the first toss is heads; so that the third case has, in fact, two options and becomes the third and fourth cases. The four possible cases are, therefore, as follows:

(a) Tails appears on the first toss and again on the second toss.
(b) Tails appears on the first toss and heads on the second toss.

(c) Heads appears on the first toss and again on the second toss.

(d) Heads appears on the first toss and tails on the second toss.

As there are now proved to be four cases and as three of these are favourable, then the probability of heads at least once is, in fact, 3/4.

103. Jugs

To solve this puzzle you must first investigate the only two possibilities by which you can begin the decanting: you can either pour water into jug B until jug B is full, or pour water into jug C until jug C is full. During the operations you must avoid a situation in which both B and C are entirely full because then the only way to proceed would be to pour the contents of B and C entirely into A—in other words go back to the beginning and start again. The two possibilities are:

JUG	A	B	C	A	B	C
Commence (litres)	8	0	0	8	0	0
Operation 1	3	5	0	5	0	3
Operation 2	3	2	3	5	3	0
Operation 3	6	2	0	2	3	3
Operation 4	6	0	2	2	5	1
Operation 5	1	5	2	7	0	1
Operation 6	1	4	3	7	1	0
Operation 7	4	4	0	4	1	3
Operation 8				4	4	0

Thus it can be seen that to commence by pouring into jug B until it is full produces the solution with the least number of decantings, which is 7.

104. One-two-three

Each line of numbers describes the line above it, i.e. 1, then 1 (one) 1, then 2 (two) 1s, then 1-2, 1-1 etc. The next row is 3 1 1 3 1 2 1 1 1 3 1 2 2 1.

105. A Bottle of Wine

Hands up everyone who said £1. This is wrong, as the total of the bottle of wine will then be £11. The correct answer is 50 pence.

106. Roll-a-penny

To win, the punter's coin must fall with the centre within the shaded area (see figure below). If the centre is outside the shaded area then the coin must touch the line somewhere and is a loser.

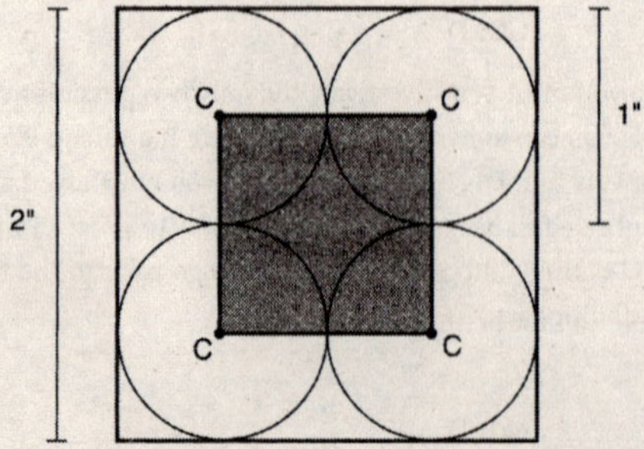

So winner area = 1 square inch; losing area = 3 square inches. Therefore the odds should be 3 to 1 and should pay out 3 times the stake plus the stake (in the case of a £.02 stake, £.08). The actual payout is $\frac{80}{16}$ = £.05. Therefore the odds favor the banker by 8 to 5.

107. The Missing £

The way the question is posed includes a piece of mathematical sleight of hand. It suggests that each man spent £9 plus £2 tip between them, but the £27 included the tip.

We should say:

The meal cost	£25
The waiter's tip	£2
Change	£3
	£30

108. Gold Card

It certainly is not! It is 2-1 on that the gambler will win. In other words, he will win 2 games out of 3.

We are not dealing with cards here but with sides. There were 6 sides to begin with, 3 of each:

GOLD	SILVER
1	
1	
	1
	1
$\frac{1}{3}$	$\frac{1}{3}$

The card on the table cannot be the silver/silver card so that variant can be eliminated. We are left with:

GOLD	SILVER
1	
1	
$\frac{1}{3}$	$\frac{1}{1}$

We can see one gold side so we are left with:

GOLD	SILVER
1	
$\frac{1}{2}$	$\frac{1}{1}$

The reverse side can be GOLD, or GOLD, or SILVER. Odds 2-1 *on.*

109. The Aeroplane

Since the wind boosts the plane's speed from A to B and retards it from B to A, one is tempted to suppose that these forces balance each other so that total travel time for the combined flights will remain the same. This is not the case, because the time during which the plane's speed is boosted is shorter than the time during which it is retarded, so the overall effect is one of retardation. The total time in a wind of constant speed and direction, regardless of the speed or direction, is always greater than if there were no wind.

110. Skiing the Globe

Suppose that three boats are needed, so that two boats can transfer their fuel at the right moment to the third. Call these A, B, and C. All three start at once from Long Beach with full tanks. When they get one-eighth of the way around, they have used up a quarter of their fuel. C then divides its fuel into three equal parts; having three-quarters of its fuel left, it transfers a quarter to A, a quarter to B, and uses the remaining quarter to return to home port. (Notice that all the fuel in its tank is used up.)

A and B now have full tanks again. They speed on till they reach a quarter of the way around. Both then have three-quarters of their fuel left. B then transfers a quarter of its fuel to A, because the remaining half is needed so that it can return to base. A full tank, we know, is sufficient to cross half-way. Since A has covered a quarter of the way with a full tank, it can cover three-quarters of the way. Here it is met by C, which, in the meantime, has refueled and sped from Long Beach in the other direction, using the fact that the Earth is round. It halves the remainder, so that both reach seven-eighths of the way, where they are met by B. To reach this point, B has used up a quarter of its fuel. It needs another quarter for the return journey, but divides the remainder between A and C. Now A, B and C can all return to base, A having successfully travelled around the Earth.

111. Four Insects

10 centimetres. Since the paths are always perpendicular to each other, the original distance remains unchanged.

112. Birth Dates

With 24 people in the room you would, in the long run, lose 23 and win 27 out of each 50 bets.

113. Changing Money

It is quite obvious that the economies of Eastland and Westland paid for the razor blades. If Malcolm were to repeat the transaction often enough, the end result would give him all, or a large part, of the stock of razor blades in both countries, together with one Eastland or Westland dollar. The two countries would be left with their stocks of blades largely denuded, but with their domestic currencies repatriated.

114. Rice Paper

The stack will clearly consist of 2^{50} sheets of paper, which is well over 17 million miles high.

115. Two Discs

It is generally argued that since the circumferences are equal, and since the circumference of A is laid out once along that of B, A must make one revolution about its own centre. But if the experiment is tried with, say, two coins of the same size, it will be found that A makes two revolutions. This fact can be shown diagrammatically as follows:

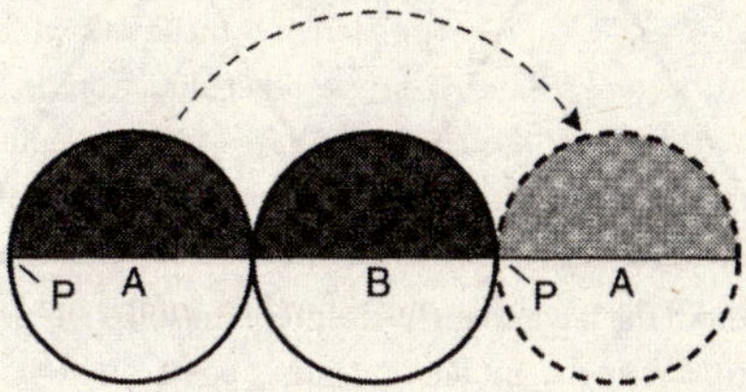

Let P be the extreme left-hand point of A when A is in its original position. A moment's thought will make it clear that when A has completed half its circuit about B, the arc of the shaded portion of A will have been laid out along that of the shaded portion of B, and P will again be the extreme left-hand point of A. Hence A must have made one revolution about its own centre. The same argument holds for the arcs of the unshaded portions of A and B when A has completed the second half of its circuit about B.

116. The Slab and the Rollers

Suppose we resolve the motion into two parts. First think of the rollers lifted off the ground and supported at their centres. Then, if the centres remain stationary, one revolution of the rollers will move the slab forward one metre. Next, think of the rollers on the ground and without the slab. Then one revolution will carry the centres of the rollers forward one metre. If now we combine these two motions, it becomes clear that one revolution of the rollers will carry the slab forward a distance of 2 metres.

117. The Broken Stick

1 chance in 4.

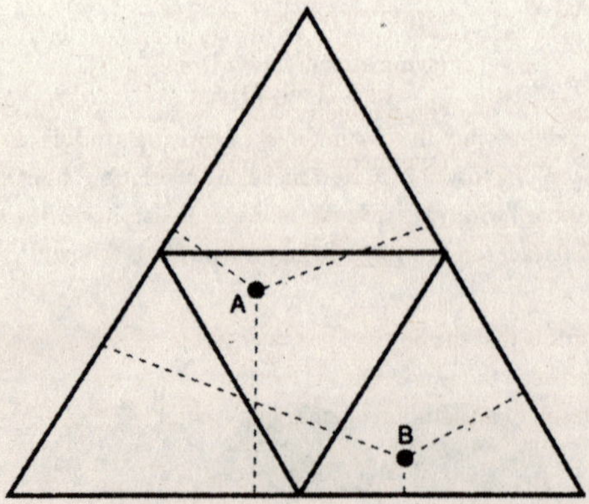

If we take any point in the large triangle, the point must fall within the smaller triangle for the 3 pieces to form a triangle. If it falls outside as point B, one side will be longer than the sum of the other 2 sides, and will not form a triangle.

118. The Slow Horses

"Change horses."

119. Hourglass

Start both hourglasses. When the 4-minute glass runs out, turn it over (4 minutes elapsed). When the 7-minute glass runs out, turn it over (7 minutes elapsed). When the 4-minute glass runs out this time (8 minutes elapsed), the 7-minute glass has been running for 1 minute. Turn it over once again. When it stops, 9 minutes have elapsed.

120. Sorting the Numbers

The numbers 15, 16 and 17 should be placed in groups 3, 3 and 2, respectively. Group 1 consists of numbers composed entirely of curved lines, Group 2 consists of numbers composed entirely of straight lines, and Group 3 consists of numbers composed of a combination of curved and straight lines.

121. Categories

The categories are as follows:

A M T U V W Y	(symmetry about vertical axis)
B C D E K	(symmetry about horizontal axis)
FGJLNPQRSZ	(no symmetry) and
H I O X	(symmetry about both axes).

122. What Weights?

1 kg, 3 kg, 9 kg.

The key to this is that the boy can put any combination of weights on either pan and the difference between the two weights is the amount of fruit he sells. Thus the weight he requires is the result of an addition or subtraction sum.

$$
\begin{aligned}
1-0 &= 1\\
3-1 &= 2\\
3-0 &= 3\\
(3+1)-0 &= 4\\
9-(3+1) &= 5\\
9-3 &= 6\\
(9+1)-3 &= 7\\
9-1 &= 8\\
9-0 &= 9\\
(9+1)-0 &= 10\\
(9+3)-1 &= 11\\
(9+3)-0 &= 12 \text{ and finally}\\
(9+3+1)-0 &= 13.
\end{aligned}
$$

123. Rope Trick

Half the rope (75 feet) plus the distance from the ground (25 feet) equal the height of the flagpoles, thus the flagpoles are right next to each other.

124. Catching the Bus

Juliette is 16⅔ or 30 metres, nearer Montreux. Lucille misses the bus everywhere.

Draw your own diagram of a straight road and letter the position of the bus B, the point where the sisters left it P, the patch of narcissi where Juliette is J, and the correct meeting point with the bus for Juliette M.

Let us call the distance PM x metres.

Juliette runs MJ metres during the time the bus travels BM metres.

$\therefore$ 2 MJ = 1 BM

But MJ = $\sqrt{40^2 + x^2}$ (Pythagoras)

and BM = $70 + x$

$$\therefore \qquad 2\sqrt{40^2 + x^2} = 70 + x$$

$$\therefore \qquad 6{,}400 + 4x^2 = 4{,}900 + 140x + x^2$$

(after squaring each side)

$$\therefore \qquad 3x^2 - 140x + 1{,}500 = 0$$

This reduces to: $(3x - 50).(x - 30) = 0$

For a product to be zero, one of its factors has to be zero

$\therefore$ Case (1) $\quad 3x - 50 = 0$ or $x = 16\frac{2}{3}$

Case (2) $\quad x - 30 = 0$ or $x = 30$

Thus Juliette could have run to a point nearer Montreux by either 16⅔ or 30 metres from the point where they left the road and she would have caught the bus.

Lucille was 41 metres from the road, therefore:

$$2\sqrt{41^2 + x^2} = 70 + x$$

which becomes:

$$4(41^2 + x^2) = 4900 + 140x + x^2$$

This reduces to:

$$3x^2 - 140x + 1824 = 0$$

This equation will not give real roots and therefore Lucille will miss the bus.

125. Bus Timetable

The buses are evenly spaced along the road in both directions. The man notices buses at the rate of 30 an hour. Because he is moving towards one "stream" of buses and away from the other, he sees more buses in one direction than the other (20 to 10), but if he were stationary he would see 15 an hour traveling each way. The buses therefore leave the terminal at 4-minute intervals.

126. How Many Hops?

You will not be able to hop out.

You hop 4½ feet at the first attempt, which is half-way out, and then another 2¼ feet at the next hop. Thus you are already three-quarters of the way out in two hops. You feel encouraged, for surely the last quarter will be hopped easily! Let us write down the hops:

$$4\tfrac{1}{2},\ 2\tfrac{1}{4},\ 1\tfrac{1}{8},\ \tfrac{9}{16},\ \tfrac{9}{32},\ \tfrac{9}{64},\ \tfrac{9}{128}, \text{ and so on.}$$

Add these up and you will see that you are nearly there—in fact, you can hop more than 8¾ feet of the total distance needed of 9 feet. But this is a series whose "sum to infinity" is less than 9 feet. You are a prisoner in the circle!

127. Decaffeine

33⅓ cups. Because there is 3 percent caffeine left in the doctored coffee; in 100 cups there would be enough for 3 cups of regular; 3 goes into 100 exactly 33⅓ times.

128. Speed Test

Let 1234567891 be n. Then the denominator can be written as:

$$n^2 - [(n-1) \times (n+1)] \text{ or } n^2 - n^2 + 1, \text{ which} = 1$$

Therefore the answer is 1234567890.

129. Walking Home

Yes. He took as much time for the second half of his trip as the whole trip would have taken on foot. So no matter how fast the train was, he lost exactly as much time as he spent on the train.

He would have saved $\frac{1}{30}$ of the time taken by walking all the way.

130. The Watchmaker

As the problem says, the apprentice mixed up the clock hands so that the minute hand was short and the hour hand long.

The first time the apprentice returned to the client was about 2 hours and 10 minutes after he had set the clock at six. The long hand moved only from 12 to a little past 2. The short hand made 2 full circles and an additional 10 minutes. Thus the clock showed the correct time.

Next day around 7:05 A.M. he came a second time, 13 hours and 5 minutes after he had set the clock for six. The long hand, acting as hour hand, covered 13 hours to reach 1. The short hand made 13 full circles and 5 minutes, reaching 7. So the clock showed the correct time again.

131. The Lead Plate

They poured the shot into the jug and then poured in water, which filled all the spaces between the pellets. Now the water volume plus the shot volume equaled the jar's volume.

Removing the shot from the jar, they measured the volume of water remaining, and subtracted it from the volume of the jar.

132. The Caliper

He placed an object (such as a strip of wood) over one end of the cylinder, then rested one leg of the caliper against that object and the other leg inside the opposite indentation. The caliper could then be removed without opening the legs. He subtracted the thickness of the object from the spread of the caliper. This gave him a measurement equal to the length of the cylinder less one indentation. Subtracting this figure from the overall length of the cylinder gave him the depth of *one* indentation; doubling this gave him the depth of both indentations, which he could then deduct from the overall length of the cylinder.

133. Fuel Tanks

Since Pete Brown takes twice as much diesel as Joe Smith, the quantity of diesel must be divisible by 3. We know that we can divide numbers by 3 only if the sum of their digits is also divisible by 3. The sum of the digits on the storage tanks gives 6, 4, 1, 2, 7, 9. The sum of all these digits is 29 (which, when divided by 3, gives the same remainder as when 11 or 2 is divided by 3).

The capacity of the tank holding the special blend of unleaded and alcohol, when subtracted from the sum of the capacities of the other barrels, should leave a number which can be divided by 3. Therefore, if the capacity of the special blend tank is divided by 3, the remainder must be 2. If we look at the capacity of the tanks, we see that only the 20-gallon tank is the right size (sum of the digits is 2); 29 – 2 = 27, which is divisible by 3. Therefore, the unleaded/alcohol blend was contained in the 20-gallon tank.

This left 99 gallons of diesel, to be divided into 33- and 66-gallon consignments for Smith and Brown respectively. Thus, Smith was given all the fuel in the 15- and 18-gallon tanks, and Brown the fuel in the 15-, 19-, and 31-gallon tanks.

134. The Wire's Diameter

Wind a number of coils tightly around a cylinder as shown on the overleaf. Twenty diameters make 2 centimeters, so one diameter is 0.1 centimeters.

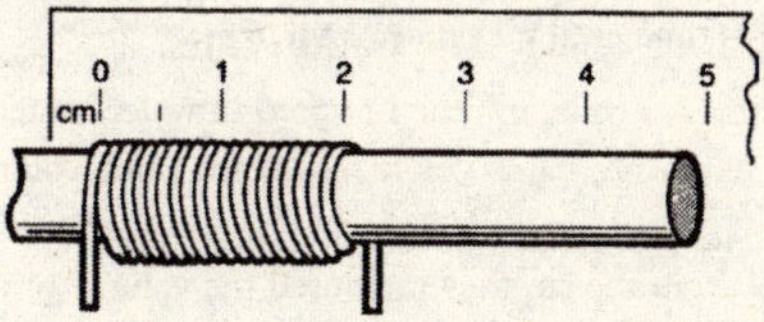

135. The Bottle's Volume

The area of circle, square or rectangle can easily be calculated after measuring sides or diameter with a rule. Call the area *s*.

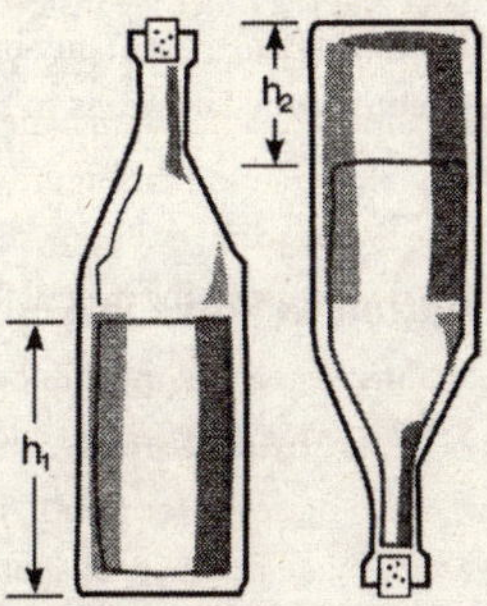

With the bottle upright (see illustration), measure the height h_1 of the liquid. The full part of the bottle has the volume sh_1

Turn the bottle upside down and measure the height h_2 of the air space. The empty part of the bottle has the volume sh_2 The whole bottle has the volume $s(h_1 + h_2)$.

136. The Ship and the Seaplane

Perhaps you can spot without any algebra or extended calculation that the seaplane goes 200 miles, while the ship goes another 20.

This is a trial-and-error exercise. Now try to solve it by equation.

Let the distance be: X

The speed of the ship: S

The speed of the seaplane 10.S,

We also know that time = distance speed = X S, then

We also know that time = $\frac{\text{distance}}{\text{speed}} = \frac{X}{S}$, then

X-180 S = X 10.S (as time until they meet is the same)

This reduces to:

10.S

$$\frac{X-180}{S} = \frac{X}{10.S}$$ (as time until they meet is the same)

This reduces to:

10.\$.x – 1800\$ = X.\$

9X = 1800

X = 200

137. The Ships and the Lifebuoy

From the buoy's point of view (floating downstream), the ships move away from it at equal speeds in still water. Then they return at equal speeds in still water. Thus the two ships reach the buoy simultaneously.

138. Equation to Solve in Your Head

Adding and subtracting the equations we see that the numbers become 10,000, 10,000 and 50,000; and 3,502, –3,502 and 3,502. Dividing by 10,000 and by 3,502 we obtain:

$$x + y = 5$$

$$x - y = 1$$

Therefore: $x = 3$

$$y = 2$$

139. Three Men in the Street

The key is that the man in white is talking to Mr. Black and so cannot be he. Nor can he be Mr. White, since nobody is wearing his own colour. So the man in white must be Mr. Gray. We can show what we know like this:

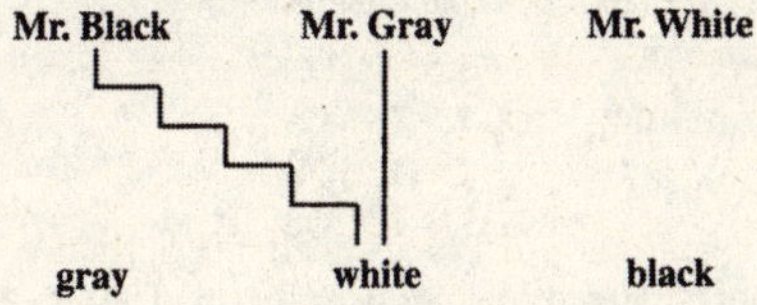

The straight line shows what must be true; the wiggly line shows what cannot be true. Mr. White cannot be wearing white; so he's in black. That leaves Mr. Black wearing gray.

140. The Square Field

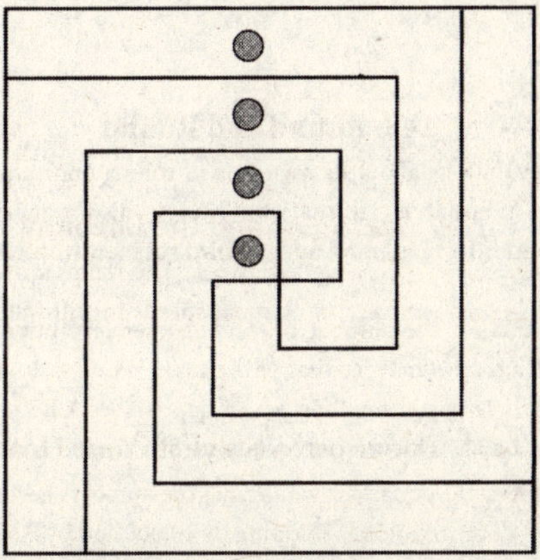

141. Kings and Queens

There are only two arrangements of Kings and Queens which can satisfy the first and second statements, these being KQQ and QKQ. The third and fourth statements are met by only two possible arrangements of Hearts and Spades, these being SSH and SHS. These two sets can be combined in four possible ways as follows:

KS, QS, QH
KS, QH, QS
QS, KS, QH
QS, KH, QS

The final set is ruled out because it contains two Queens of Spades. Since all the other sets consist of the King of Spades, Queen of Spades and Queen of Hearts, these must be the three cards on the table. It is not possible to state definitely which position any particular card is in, but the first must be a Spade and the third a Queen.

142. Even Tread

Each tyre was used for four-fifths of the total mileage: four-fifths of 10,000 miles = 8,000 miles per tyre.

143. Round and Round

Wheel A makes 3 revolutions about its own axis in rolling once around Wheel B. Since the circumference of Wheel A is half that of Wheel B, this produces two rotations with respect to Wheel B, and the revolution adds a third rotation with respect to an observer from above.

The general formula for the number of rotations per revolution is (B/A) + 1. So, if rolling Wheel A had a diameter twice that of the fixed Wheel B, it would rotate one and a half times. As it gets larger, the rolling wheel approaches a limit of one rotation per revolution, this limit being achieved only when it rolls around a degenerate "circle" (or point) of zero diameter.

144. Choose a Glass

The binary procedure is the most efficient method for testing any number of glasses of liquid in order to identify a single glass containing poison. First the glasses are divided as nearly in half as possible. Then one set is tested by taking a sample from each glass, combining them, and testing the mixture. The set identified as including the poisoned glass is then divided again as nearly in half as possible, and the procedure repeated until the poisoned glass is identified. If the number of glasses is between 100 and 128 inclusive, as many as 7 tests might be required. From 129 to 200 glasses might take 8 tests. The number 128 is the turning point. Since we know that the number was between 100 and 200 there must therefore have been 129 glasses in the hotel lounge, because only in that case would the initial testing of one glass make no difference in applying the most efficient testing procedure. To test 129 glasses by halving could result in 8 tests. If a single glass were tested first the remaining 128 glasses would require no more than 7 tests, so that the total number of tests remains the same.

When the above answer was first published, many people wrote to say that the detective inspector was right, and the statistician wrong. Regardless of the number of glasses, the most efficient testing procedure is to divide them as nearly in half as possible at each step and test the glasses in either set. When the probabilities are worked out, the expected number of tests of 129 glasses, if the halving procedure is followed, is 7.0155+. But if a single glass is tested first, the expected number is 7.9457+. This is an increase of 0.930+ test, so the inspector was almost right in considering the statistician to be wasting one test.

Put in simple terms, the statistician's suggestion would result in a wasted test in every case other than if the suspect glass happened to be the last one— the 129th—tested, and the chance of that occurring at random is not high.

145. The Square Window

See the illustration. The shaded area is the part of the window that is painted blue.

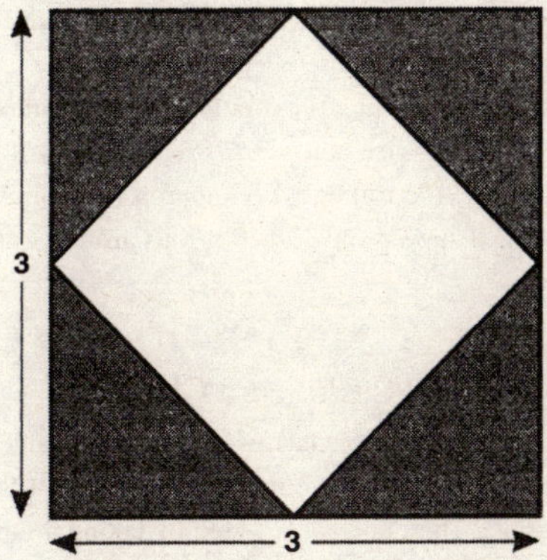

146. Dominoes

You can solve this with pages of diagrams and calculations—or, by an insightful shortcut, in just a couple of sentences. Every domino must cover 2 adjacent squares—that is, one black square and one white square. The diagonally opposite squares on a draughts board are of the same colour, both white in our example. You can arrange 30 dominoes so that they cover all 30 white squares and 30 of the black, but there will always be 2 black squares left, and the one remaining domino can't cover them both.

147. A Bridge Game

FLUSH: the two events are equally likely. You may prove this by doing pages of calculations or by using shortcut reasoning. If two players hold all the cards in one suit, the other two players are necessarily void in that suit—the two events occur together, hence they are equally probable.

PAPER PERFECT: All stories of perfect deals in bridge should be taken with a large pinch of salt. The odds against one are 2,235,197,406,985,633,368,301,599,999 to 1. This is so remote that a perfect deal has probably never occurred by chance (as opposed to by dint of a prank or a poorly shuffled deck) in the entire history of the game. If everyone in the world were dealt 60 bridge hands a day, a perfect deal would occur only once in 124 trillion years!

148. Computers

Three computers.

149. A Third of the Planet

You would have to be at a distance equal to the Earth's diameter—about 7,900 miles.

Imagine Earth to be a circle instead of a sphere:

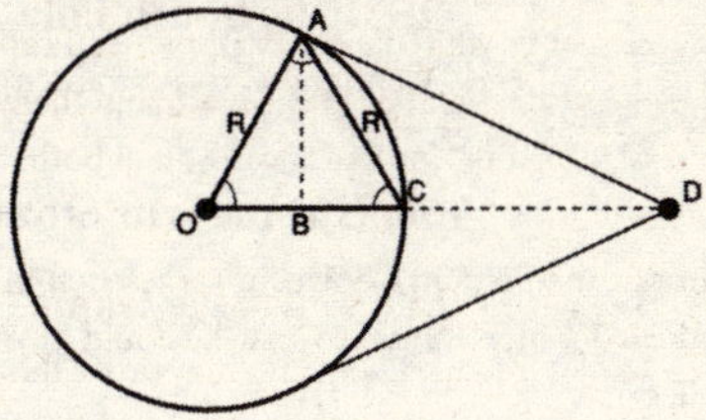

$\triangle$ OAC is equilateral.

$\triangle$ OAB is similar to $\triangle$ OAD. $OD{:}R = \frac{R}{2}$

$R^2 = OD{:}\ \frac{R}{2}$ or $OD = 2R$

150. Checkers

Take the 2 draughts shown below in the illustration, and shift them to positions at right, pushing their respective rows backwards to make the columns align.

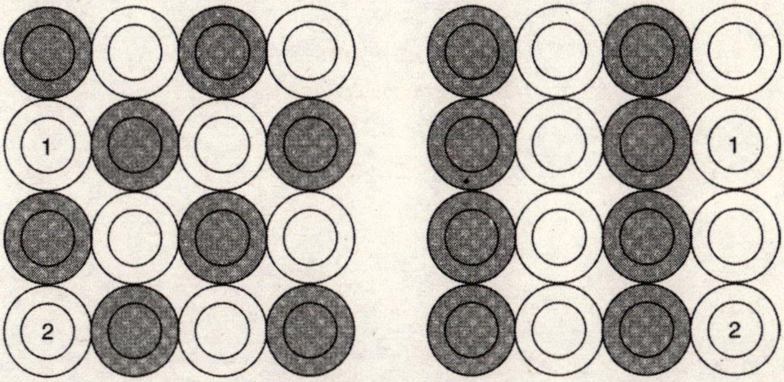

151. The Handicap Race

Mel wins again. In the second race, after Sid has gone 90 yards, Mel will have gone 100, and they will be alongside each other. There are 10 more yards to run, and since Mel is the faster runner, he will finish first.

152. ... 9, 10

9 below, 10 above. Numbers appearing above the line are spelled with 3 letters only.

153. The South Pole

–40° Centigrade = –40° Fahrenheit.

154. Guinness or Stout

The second man put the 50 pence down in some combination of change—for instance, 4×10 pence and 2×5 pence coins—so that he could have put just 45 pence down if he had wanted Jubilee.

155. Bonus Payments

Let m be the number of men and let x be the fraction of men refusing a bonus. Then the amount paid out is given by

$$T = 8.15(350 - m) + 10(1 - x)m = 2852.50 + m(1.85 - 10x)$$

which will be independent of m only if $x = 0.185$, so that $T = 2852.50$. Both m and $0.185m$ are integers with $m < 350$, so $m = 200$. It follows that £1,222.50 is paid to the 150 women.

156. The Tiled Floor

To fall and not touch a line the card must fall so that the centre of the card falls within the shaded area.

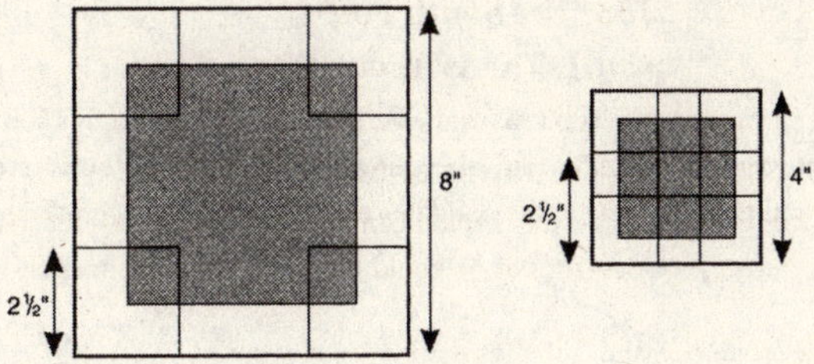

	For		Against
Therefore	$30\frac{1}{4}$	–	$33\frac{3}{4}$
	$2\frac{1}{4}$	–	$13\frac{3}{4}$
	$2\frac{1}{4}$	–	$13\frac{3}{4}$
	$2\frac{1}{4}$	–	$13\frac{3}{4}$
	$2\frac{1}{4}$	–	$13\frac{3}{4}$
	$39\frac{1}{4}$	–	$88\frac{3}{4}$

$\times 4$ to remove fractions = 157 to 355 against.

157. A Shuffled Deck

The number of red cards in the top 26 must always equal the number of black cards in the bottom 26. Hence, by the rules of logic, the statement is correct no matter what follows the word "then!"

158. A Peculiar Number

The common result must have 7 and 11 as factors, thus the number is 7 + 11 or 18. The method is general, since the solution of $(x - k)k = (x - m)m$ is $k + m$.

159. Antifreeze

One quart of the old solution differs from one quart of the new (or average) solution by –24 percent, while one quart of the solution to be added differs from the new solution by +48 percent. Hence, there must be 2 quarts of the old solution for each quart of the added solution. So a third of the original radiator content or 7 quarts must be drained.

160. Tree Leaves

If it be required that no tree be completely devoid of leaves, then the statement would be true.

161. The Will

Daniel Greene's evident intention was that his estate be divided 2 : 1 between his son and his widow, or 1 : 3 between his daughter and his widow. These ratios can be preserved by giving the son six-tenths of the estate, the daughter one-tenth, and his widow, Sheila, three-tenths.

Let the value of the estate be S and Sheila's share x
Boy's share y
Girl's share z

By definition Sheila is to receive half of the boy's share and three times the girl's share, or

$$x = \frac{y}{2}, \quad x = 3z$$

But $x + y + z = s$ or

$$x + 2x + \frac{x}{3} = s$$

$$\therefore \quad \frac{3x}{3} + \frac{6x}{3} + \frac{x}{3} = \frac{3s}{3}, \qquad \therefore\ 10x = s$$

The estate is therefore shared

Mother	$\frac{3}{10}$
Boy	$\frac{6}{10}$
Girl	$\frac{1}{10}$

162. Watered-down Wine

There is exactly as much water in the wine jug as there is wine in the water jug. Regardless of the proportions of wine and water which have been transferred, if both jugs originally held equal volumes of unadulterated liquids and both are eventually left the equal volumes of mixtures, then equal amounts of wine and water must have been transferred.This old brainteaser also forms the basis of a perplexing card trick: The performer and the spectator are seated opposite each other at a table. The performer turns 20 cards face-up from a pack of 52 cards. The spectator is asked to shuffle the pack so that the reversed cards are randomly distributed, then to hold the pack out of sight beneath the table and to count off 20 cards from the top. These 20 cards are passed, under the table, to the performer.

Having taken the 20 cards, the performer continues to hold them beneath the table, and tells the spectator: "Neither of us knows how many reversed cards there are in this pack of 20. However it is likely that there are fewer reversed cards in the pack of 20 than there are in the pack of 32 which you are holding. Without looking at my cards, I am going to turn some more face-down cards face-up in an attempt to equalize the number of reversed cards in my packet with the number in yours."

The performer then fiddles with his packet of cards under the table, making out that he can feel the difference between fronts and backs. After a few moments, he brings them into view and spreads them on the table. When the faceup cards are counted, it turns out that their number is exactly the same as the number of face-up cards in the spectator's packet of 32. What he's done, of course, is just turn his entire stack of 20 cards over!

163. A Logic Riddle

The answer is 4. The problem can be written by way of analogy as follows:

$$\frac{5}{2} : 3 = \frac{10}{3} : x$$

$$\therefore x = 4$$

An alternative reasoning goes as follows:

If 2½ = 3, then 10 = 12

Therefore ⅓ of 10 would be 4

164. A Matter of Health

If there were just two ailments with the percentages 70 percent and 75 percent, then the minimum overlap would be 45 percent, or 70 percent plus 75 percent minus 100. The minimum 45 percent of the population with the first two conditions similarly overlaps the 80 percent with the third ailment by a minimum of 25 percent. Finally the minimum of 25 percent suffering from the first three ailments overlaps the 85 percent with the fourth condition by at least 10 percent. The same principle would apply to any other combination of any number of ailments. The answer can be calculated instantly with the following formula:

$$(A1\% + A2\% + A3\% + \ldots An\%) - 100 \times (N - 1) = 10\%$$

where Al . . . An are the percentages of the various ailments and N is the number of different ailments.

165. Tramlines

The solution normally given to this problem uses the method of relative speeds: the relative velocity between man and tram when going in the same and opposite directions respectively is proportional to the number of trams encountered. This establishes the equation:

$$(x + 3)(x - 3) = \tfrac{60}{40}$$

Therefore $x = 15$ miles per hour.

However, a simpler explanation that short-circuits the algebra is this: picture two trams at the start of the walk, the 40th tram behind the man and the 60th ahead of him. These must have each travelled half the distance between them when they met at the man, namely, a 50-tram space. So the distance walked in the same period was a 10-tram space, or one-fifth as much, which means the speed of the tram was 15 miles per hour.

166. Passing Trains

If it takes 10 seconds for a train of length L to pass A, and 9 seconds to pass B, the relative velocity between the train and A is L/10, between the train and B is L/9, and between A and B is L/90. The latter figure is one-tenth the relative velocity between the train and B. Since it took the train 1,210 seconds to reach B, it will take A ten times as long, or 12,100 seconds, of which 1,219 seconds had elapsed when the train passed B, leaving 3 hours, 1 minute and 21 seconds.

An alternative, and perhaps more interesting, solution considers an observer looking out of a supposedly stationary train at the two walkers. It appears to such an observer that the woman moves faster than the man, since the woman takes 9 seconds to cover a distance that the man covers in 10 seconds, and thus in a 9-second period the woman gains 1 second over the man. It is given that the woman goes past the rear end of the train 20 minutes and 9 seconds after the man, and for them to meet it would take 9 times this interval, or 3 hours, 1 minute and 21 seconds.

167. The Fly and the Record

It will arrive at the outer edge. When a record is played on a turntable, it revolves clockwise when seen from above, and relative to the record, the needle moves anticlockwise as seen from above. If the needle—and hence the fly—were to move clockwise around the groove, it would end up at the outer edge.

168. Move One Coin

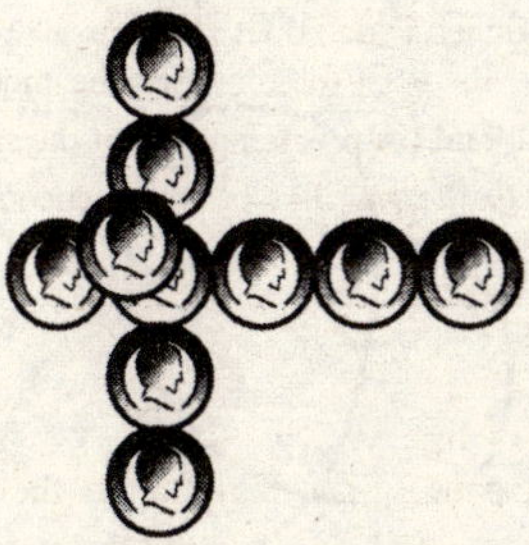

Simply place one coin on top of another at the intersection of the two rows.

169. The Unbalanced Coin

An unbalanced coin can be used to generate a series of truly random numbers. In trying to determine each number, toss the coin twice. Since the coin is biased, the outcome heads-heads (HH) will not occur with the same frequency as tails-tails (TT). But the sequence HT is as likely as TH, no matter how unfair the coin may be. You simply flip the coin twice for each trial, rejecting both HH and TT, then designate HT as “one” and TH as “zero” (or vice versa).

170. Bicycle Experiment

Strange as it may seem, pulling back on the lower pedal causes the bicycle to move backwards. The force on the pedal is in the direction that would normally propel the bicycle forward, but the large size of the wheels and the small gear ratio between the pedal and the wheel sprockets are such that the bicycle is free to move backward with the pull. When it does so, the pedal actually moves forward with respect to the bicycle (that is, in an anticlockwise direction in the illustration), although it moves backwards with respect to the ground.

The higher pedal, if pulled back, would simply free-turn until it reached the point in its arc closest to the source of the pulling-force, at which point the bike would move backwards.

171. A Piece of String

Assume that at A the string going from top left to bottom right is on top. (If it is the other way a mirror solution is produced which does not alter the probability.)

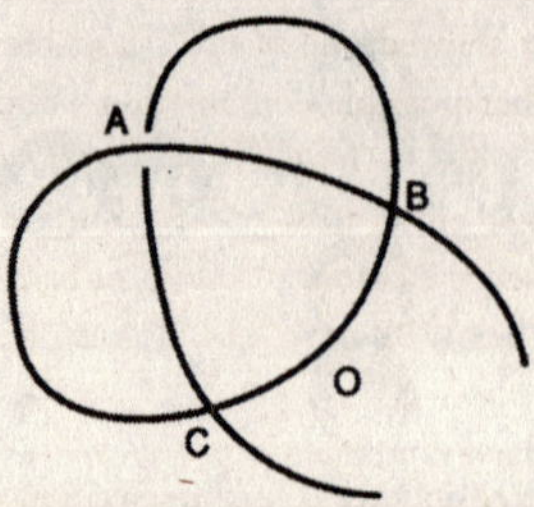

Then we have four equal possibilities. The segment BOC can be either on top or underneath at each of the points B and C.

Segment BOC		
At B	*At C*	*The string is*
On top	On top	Not knotted
On top	Under	Not knotted
Under	On top	Knotted
Under	Under	Not knotted

Hence the chance that the string forms a knot is 1 in 4.

172. The Island and the Trees

The girl ties one end of the rope to the tree at the edge of the lake. She walks around the lake holding the other end of the rope, then ties that end to the same tree. The doubled rope is now firmly stretched between the two trees, making it easy for her to pull herself through the water, by means of the rope, to the island.

173. A Boy, a Girl and a Dog

The dog can be at any point between the boy and the girl, facing either way. To prove this, at the end of one hour place the dog anywhere between the boy and the girl, facing in either direction. Reverse all the motions, and all three will return at the same instant to the starting point.

174. Boxes and Balls

Once a girl removed 2 balls from her box, she narrowed the possible combinations in her box to 2. If she was able to deduce the colour of the third ball, it must have been because the label on her box showed one of the 2 possible combinations, forcing the actual contents to be the other possible combination—remember, all the boxes were incorrectly labelled.

The first girl's box contained either BBB or WBB, and its label must have read WBB or BBB for her to have guessed the colour of the third ball. Similarly, the second girl's box must have contained either WBB or WBW, with its label reading either WBW or WBB.

The third girl's box must have contained either WWW or WBW—but her box could not have been labelled either of these, otherwise she, too, would have been able to deduce the colour of her third ball.

The only distribution satisfying all these conditions is:

Girl	*1*	*2*	*3*	*4*
Label	WBB	WBW	BBB	
Actual	BBB	WBB	?	

The fourth girl instantly realized that her box must be labeled WWW; since it could not actually have contained WWW, the third girl's box must have contained that combination, leaving her (the fourth girl's) box to contain WBW.

175. Two Trains

The passenger train is 3 times as fast as the freight train. Using the formula:

$$\text{Time (T)} = \frac{\text{Distance (D)}}{\text{Speed (S)}}$$

Let X be the speed of the passenger train, and
Let Y be the speed of the freight train, and
Let T1 and T2 be the time taken for passing (overtaking and meeting respectively), then:

$$T1 = \frac{D}{X-Y} \text{ and } T2 = \frac{D}{X+Y}\text{, also}$$

$T1 = 2 \times T2$, therefore:

$$\frac{D}{X-Y} = \frac{2.D}{X+Y} \quad \text{D cancels out, leaving:}$$

$$\frac{1}{X-Y} = \frac{2}{X+Y} \quad \text{This simplifies to } X+Y = 2X-2Y\text{, leaving:}$$

$$X = 3Y$$

176. Missing Elevation

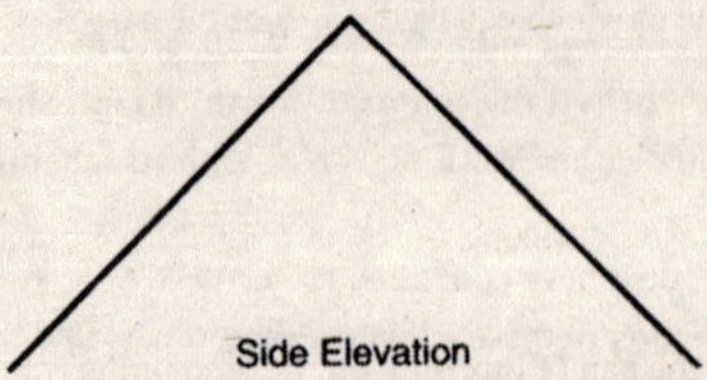

This is a wire figure, in the form of an ellipse, bent at its smaller "diameter."

177. Avoiding the Train

The stretch of track the man was walking on was over a railway bridge or in a tunnel, and he was much nearer the end closer to the train than the farther end.

178. Bowl and Pan

She fills the pan on the table more than half full, and then carefully tilts up one end, pouring out the water, until the level reaches E, the bottom edge of the raised end (Figure 1). This leaves exactly half a litre in the pan, since the empty part is the same shape and size as the filled part.

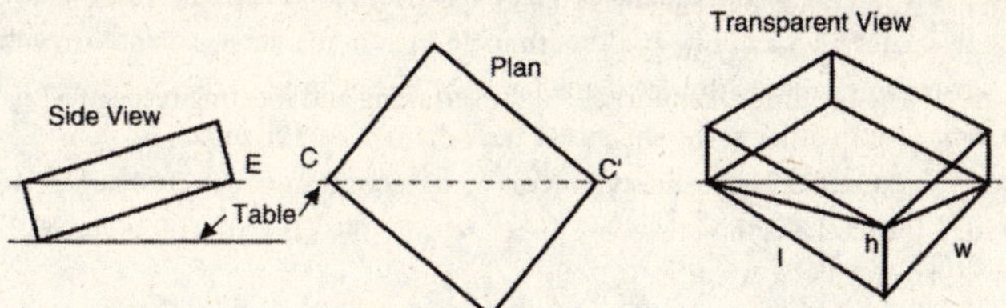

Figure 1 Figure 2 Figure 3

The table has a straight edge, and mother slides the pan over the edge so that the opposite corners C and *C* coincide with the edge (Figure 2). She starts tilting again, with the bowl held to catch the water, and tilts until the surface of the water coincides with the corners C and C. The bowl now contains one-third of a litre. Proof: If the proportions of the pan are ignored, Figure 3 shows the pan at the end of pouring. The remaining water is in the form of a pyramid, the volume of which equals the area of the base times one-third its height.

$$\text{Area of base} = \frac{1w}{2}$$

$$\therefore \quad \text{volume} = \frac{1w}{2} \times \frac{h}{3} = \frac{1wh}{6}$$

Since the volume of the pan (1 litre) = 1 *wh*, the remaining water = one-sixth of a litre. Thus, she poured into the bowl one-half less one-sixth of a litre, or one-third of a litre.

179. Jasmin's Age

Jasmin's age was 22 years and 8 months.

Let Jasmin's real age be "*x*."

She reduced her real age by ¼ minus 1 year.

$$\therefore \left(\frac{x}{4} - 1\right) + 18 = x \text{ or}$$

$$x - 4 + 72 = 4x$$

Reduce to

$$3x = 68 \quad \text{or} \quad x = 22\tfrac{2}{3} = 22 \text{ years and 8 months}$$

180. A Ball of Wire

This problem can be solved by reference to Archimedes' discovery that the volume of a sphere is two-thirds the volume of a cylindrical box into which the sphere exactly fits. The ball of wire has a diameter of 24 inches, so its volume is the same as that of a cylinder with height 16 inches and base diameter 24 inches.

Since wire is simply an extended cylinder, it is necessary to calculate how many pieces of wire 16 inches high and one-hundredth of an inch in diameter are equal in volume to a 16-inch-high cylinder with base diameter of 24 inches. Areas of circles are in the same proportion to each other as the squares of their diameters. The square of $\frac{1}{100}$ is $\frac{1}{10000}$, and the square of 24 is 576. Hence the cylinder is equal in volume to 5,760,000 of the 16-inch-long wires. The total length of the wire, therefore, is 5,760,000 × 16, or 92,160,000 inches = 1,454 miles and 2,880 feet.

181. Ferry Boats

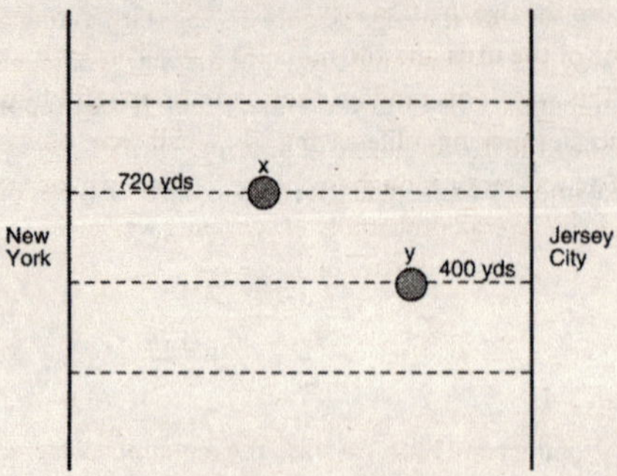

When the ferry boats meet at point X, they are 720 yards from one shore. The combined distance that both have travelled is equal to the width of the river. When they reach the opposite shore, the combined distance is equal to twice the width of the river. On the return trip, they meet at point Y after travelling a combined distance of 3 times the width of the river, so each boat has gone 3 times as far as they had when they first met.

At the first meeting, one boat had gone 720 yards, so when it reaches Z it must have gone three times that distance = 2,160 yards. This distance is 400 yards more than the river's width, which must therefore be 2,160 – 400 = 1,760 yards or 1 mile wide.

182. John and the Chicken

First, determine how far John would travel to catch the chicken if the chicken and John both ran forward in a straight line. Add to this the distance that John would travel to catch the chicken if they ran towards each other in a straight line. Divide the result by 2 and you have the distance that John travels.

In this case, the chicken is 250 yards away, and the speeds of John and the chicken are in the proportion of 4 to 3. So, if both ran forward in a straight line, John would travel 1,000 yards to overtake the chicken. If they travelled towards each other, John would travel four-sevenths of 250, or $142^{6}/_{7}$ yards. Adding the two distances and dividing by 2 gives us $571\frac{3}{7}$ yards for the distance travelled by John. Since the chicken runs at three-quarters the speed of John, it will have travelled three-quarters of John's distance, or $428^{4}/_{7}$ yards.

183. The Prisoner's Choice

The prisoner believed he could improve his chances by distributing the gold and silver balls unevenly between the two urns. In fact, he decided his best strategy was to place just one silver ball in one of the urns and the remaining 49 silver balls and all 50 gold balls in the second urn. This way, if his random choice of urn brought him the second urn to pick from, his chances of picking a life-saving silver ball were only slightly worse than 1-2 (49-99), while if he was lucky enough to choose the first urn, he was certain to escape death. In this manner, his overall probability of surviving was

$$\frac{1}{2} \times 1 + \frac{1}{2} \times \frac{49}{99} - \frac{74}{99}$$

or a little less than 3-4.

184. Counters in a Cup

There is no ordinary way in which the counters can be distributed to solve the problem, so there must be a catch. It lies in the ambiguity of how one thing can be placed "inside" another. The solution requires that one cup, containing an odd number of counters, be placed inside another cup (initially containing an even number of counters, which number is rendered "odd" by the counters in the inset cup). The illustration shows one of several ways in which the desired result can be achieved.

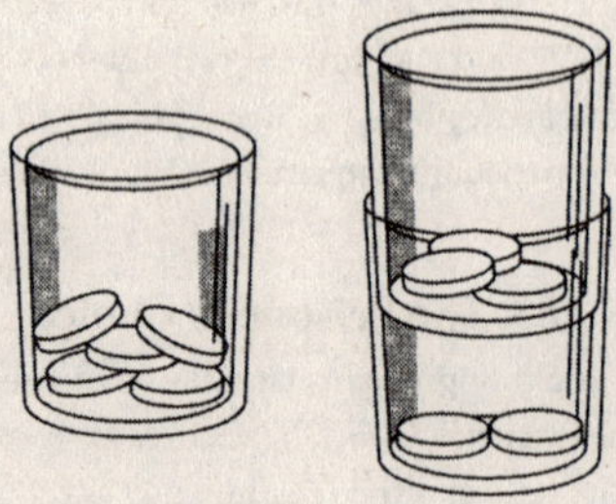

185. Speed of Ant

The ant is approaching Kings Cross at 181 centimetres per second. It doesn't matter how fast the man eats. Since the ant is walking away from his mouth at 1 cm per second—i.e. 3 cm per second relative to the hot dog—it is moving towards the station 1 cm per second faster than the man is.

186. Wayne and Shirley

Most people think that two of each is more likely. But the correct answer is in fact three of one sex and one of the other. Set out below are all the possible combinations of four children:

B B B B	
B B B G	one girl
B B G B	
B G B B	
G B B B	
G G G B	one boy
G G B G	
G B G G	
B G G G	
B B G G	two of each
B G B G	
B G G B	
G B B G	
G B G B	
G G B B	
G G G G	

Each of the 16 arrangements is equally likely. In eight cases, there is a three-one split, whereas in only six cases is there a two-two split.

187. Word Series

The answer is (d) *heaven.* The sequence of ordinal numbers is implied: first aid, second nature, Third World, Fourth Estate, Fifth Column, sixth sense, seventh heaven.

188. Shooting Match

No. Bill and Ben's overall shooting performance was the same. Accuracy ratings are calculated from the ratio of hits to attempts. Bill's rating was 28/84 and Ben's was 25/75, so the two men tied because each hit the target with one third of his shots.

189. Lethargic Llamas

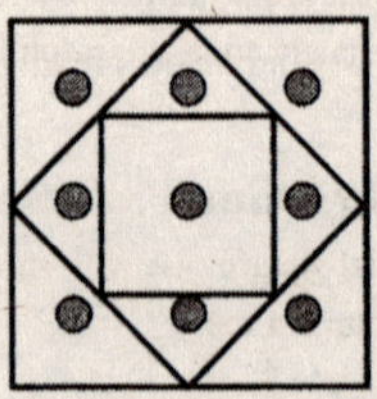

Two more square pens can be positioned as shown to give each llama its own enclosure.

190. Torpid Tapirs

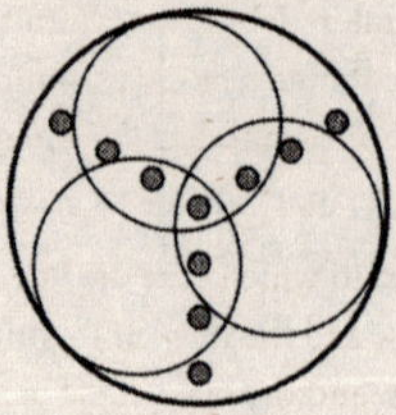

Three overlapping circular enclosures can be positioned as shown to separate the tapirs.

191. Wooden Block

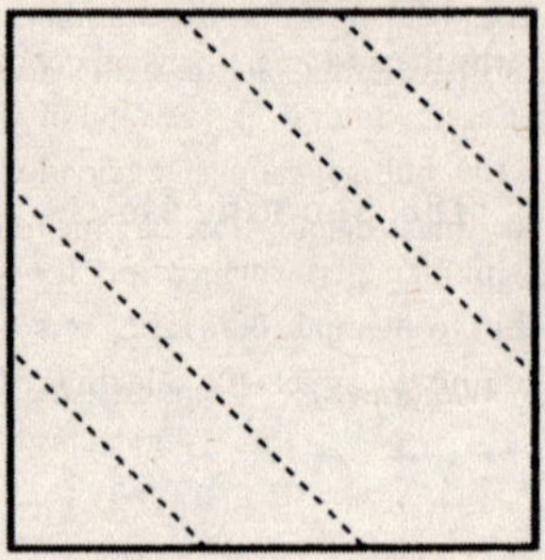

Diagonal grooves were cut in the wooden block as shown above. The two pieces could then slide apart diagonally.

192. Word Affinity

With the exception of SOCK, all the words in the two rows can be prefixed by AIR. (The prefix for SOCK that most immediately comes to mind is WIND.)

193. Gun Problem

I packed my gun diagonally in a flat square case with sides 1 metre long. The length of the diagonal was $\sqrt{2}$ metre or more than 1.4 metre.

194. Counter Colours

Most people think that because the state of the bag after the removal of the white counter is exactly the same as it was before the white counter was put in, the probability must be 1-2. This is not, however, the case.

The odds of the original counter (let's call it Counter *x*) in the bag being black or white are even. Adding a white counter (call this Counter *y*) makes the odds of the bag containing 2W or WB even. After one white counter is removed, three possibilities present themselves:

a) The counter removed was *x*, in which case the one left is certainly white.

b) The counter removed was *y*, and the one left is white.

c) The counter removed was *y*, and the one left is black.

In two out of the above three possible cases, the counter left in the bag is white; so the odds are 2 : 1 in favour of the second counter being white.

195. Bank Account

There is no reason whatever why the customer's original deposit of £100 should equal the total of the balances left after each withdrawal. The total of withdrawals in the left-hand column must always equal £100, but it is purely coincidence that the total of the right-hand column is close to £100. This is demonstrated by the following example, showing a different pattern of withdrawals:

Withdrawls	*Balance left*
£5	£95
£5	£90
£90	£0
£100	£185

196. Hat In the River

Because the rate of flow of the river has the same effect on both the boat and the hat, it can be ignored. Instead of the water moving and the shore remaining fixed, imagine the water as perfectly still and the shore moving. As far as the boat and the hat are concerned, this situation is exactly the same as before. Since the man rows 5 miles away from the hat, then 5 miles back, he has rowed a total distance of 10 miles with respect to the water. Since his rowing speed with respect to the water is 5 miles an hour, it must have taken him 2 hours to go the 10 miles. He would therefore recover his hat at 4 o'clock.

197. Tossing Pennies

No, it would be very unwise of Jack to accept the bet. To find the chances that the 3 coins will fall alike, consider all the possible ways that the 3 coins can fall, as follows:

1: H H H
2: H H T
3: H T H
4: H T T
5: T H H
6: T H T
7: T T H
8: T T T

Each of the 8 possibilities is equally likely to occur.

Note that only 2 of them show all the coins alike.

This means that the chances of all 3 coins being alike are 2 out of 8, or one quarter. There are 6 ways that the coins can fall without being all alike. Therefore the chances that this will happen are three-quarters.

In other words, Jill would expect in the long run to win 3 times out of every 4 tosses. For these wins Jack would pay her £1.50. For the one time that Jack would win, she would pay him £1. This gives Jill a profit of 50 pence for every 4 tosses on average.

198. The Kings

Let the 6 cards be numbered 1 to 6, and assume that the two Kings are cards 5 and 6. Now list all the different combinations of 2 cards that can be picked from 6, as follows:

1–2	2–3	3–4	4–5	5–6
1–3	2–4	3–5	4–6	
1–4	2–5	3–6		
1–5	2–6			
1–6				

Note that the Kings (cards 5 and 6) appear in 9 out of the 15 pairs. Since each pair is equally likely, this means that in the long run a King will be turned up in 9 out of every 15 tries. So the chances of getting a King are three-fifths. This of course is better than one-half, so the answer is that (a) is more likely.

199. Traffic Lights

The answer is ⅛, ¼, ⅜, ¼, ⅛

Since Robert travelled through the whole system in less than 2 minutes, the total distance is less than 2½ miles, and no section is longer than 1¾ miles. If we chart the three arrival times at all possible positions of the first light (green from 3-16 seconds, 29–42 seconds, etc.), the only one allowing all three to pass is ⅛ mile:

First light	Arrival time at 30 m.p.h.	Arrival time at 50 m.p.h.	Arrival time at 75 m.p.h.
$\frac{1}{8}$	15 seconds	9 seconds	6 seconds
$\frac{1}{4}$	30 seconds	18 seconds (RED)	
$\frac{3}{8}$	45 seconds (RED)		
$\frac{1}{2}$	60 seconds	36 seconds	24 seconds (RED)
$\frac{5}{8}$	75 seconds (RED)		
$\frac{3}{4}$	90 seconds	54 seconds (RED)	

Robert arrives at the last light just as it changes. A table of each ⅛ mile together with the light sequence times of traffic lights (should they be situated there) shows that the only distance where a light change coincides with Robert's arrival is 1¼ miles after the start. (For example, a light at ¼ of a mile after the start would have green showing 15 seconds later than at the first light, and a light at ⅜ of a mile would have green showing 30 seconds later, and so on.)

The same chart shows that, as Robert is not stopped, there is no light at ¼, ⅝ or 1 mile from the start. The information about Hubert enables the rest of the distances to be calculated.

200. The Feast Day

Assume there are n days between consecutive Feast Days, that the temple bell rings every x minutes, and the monastery bell rings every $x + p$ minutes. Since the two bells alternate, the situation is as follows:

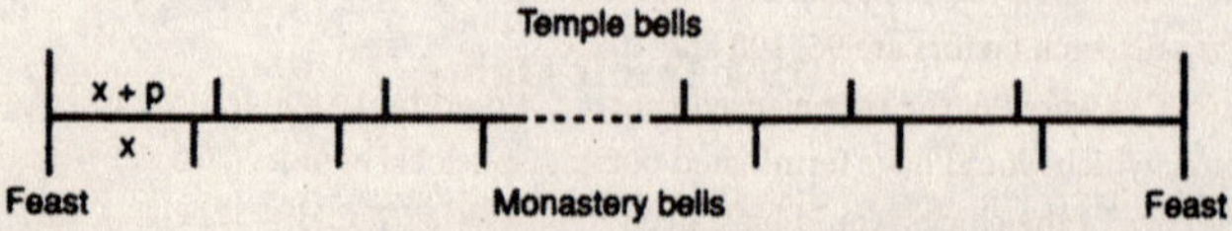

The pauses between successive rings are p, 2p, 3p, ..., 3p, 2p, p. Since one of these is 1 minute, it follows that p = 1. Since the first temple bell is 1 minute after the monastery bell, the second temple bell is 2 minutes after the monastery bell, and the xth temple bell is x minutes after the xth monastery bell.

Therefore, in the $n \times 24 \times 60$ minutes between Feast Days, there are exactly x intervals of $x + 1$ minutes. Hence $x(x + 1) = 1440 \times n$.

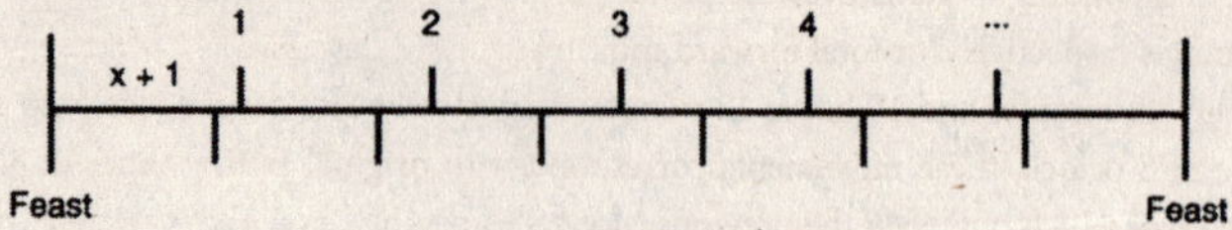

The problem is therefore to find a prime number n such that $1440 \times n$ is the product of two consecutive integers. The obvious candidates are $n= 1439$ and $n = 1441$, and indeed 1439 is prime. Hence the answer is 1,439 days.

201. The Clock-mender

The answer is 9:48 A.M. on the previous Monday.

We know from the question that the period of observation must be less than 8 days, and since the two clocks are known to be keeping different times and gaining or losing less than 60 minutes per day, they cannot both be gaining or both losing, for the faster clock could not overtake the slower clock by 12 hours in so short a period. Hence one clock must be gaining by, say, x minutes per day, and the other losing by, say, y minutes per day. Thus after a true elapsed time of m minutes, the two clocks will have moved forward respectively by:

$$m \times \frac{1440 + x}{1440} \text{ and } m \times \frac{1440 - y}{1440}$$

minutes. For both to show the same hour, the difference between these two movements must equal 12 hours or some multiple thereof, i.e.:

$$\frac{m(x+y)}{1440} - 720 \text{ etc. or } m - \frac{720 \times 1440}{(x+y)} \text{ etc.}$$

Since m is known to be an integer and less than 8×1440 minutes, $(x + y)$ must be a factor of 720×1440, which exceeds 90 but is less than 120, since x and y are each less than 60. The only such factors are 96, 100 and 108.

If $(x + y)$ were 96, the true elapsed time, m, would be 10,800 minutes, or 7 days plus 12 hours, which would have terminated outside the clock-mender's working hours so the coincidence of the clocks would have been unobserved. Similarly if $(x + y)$ were 108, the true elapsed time would be 9,600 minutes or 6 days plus 16 hours, which again would have terminated outside working hours, since 5:00 P.M. to 9:30 A.M. is already 16½ hours. Thus $(x + y)$ can only be 100, giving a true elapsed time of 7.2×1440 minutes, or $7^1/_5$ days. Since both clocks have moved forward an exact number of minutes, both x and y must be multiples of 5.

The alternatives, therefore, for the clock which is gaining are 55, 50 or 45 minutes per day, corresponding to gains over the period of 6 hours 36 minutes, 6 hours, and 5 hours 24 minutes respectively, or total forward movements of (7 days plus) 11 hours 24 minutes, 10 hours 48 minutes and 10 hours 12 minutes respectively. Since the clocks were showing a time of 8 o'clock, these movements correspond with original setting times of 8.36, 9:12 and 9:48, of which only 9:48 the previous Monday morning lies within the clock-mender's working hours.

202. The Bridge

Michael set out for B-town as soon as he saw the sentry disappear into his bunker. Timing his progress, he walked for almost 5 minutes. He then turned round and started running back towards A-town. The sentry emerged and, seeing Michael running towards A-town, ordered him to "return" to B-town.

203. The Cookie Jar

While this is ostensibly a "trial-and-error" exercise, a systematic approach is possible. Let us assume, in turn, that each child has stolen the cookie, and see whether the other statements are then compatible with the condition that three are lies and only one statement is true. If Ann is the thief, her statement is a lie; Harry's statement is a lie; Lisa's statement is true; Fred's statement is true. Therefore this cannot be the solution.

In practice, it saves time to test the person who makes a statement about herself—in this case Lisa. If Lisa is the thief, then Ann's statement is a lie; Harry's statement is a lie; Lisa's statement is a lie; Fred's statement is true.

204. Crossing the Desert

Each man will have: 2 full bottles, 1 half-full bottle, and 2 empty bottles.

Reasoning: There is enough water for 7½ full bottles. There are 15 bottles altogether. Therefore each man will end up with 2½ full bottles and 2½ empty bottles. However, half an empty bottle is the same as half a full bottle, leading to the above result.

205. Panama Canal

The west end of the Panama Canal is in fact in the Caribbean and the east end is in the Pacific. The confusion arises because the isthmus curves around at that point. As can be seen from any atlas, the canal runs from north-west to south-east.

206. The Short Cut

At 40 miles per hour, the train would enter the tunnel when John was still two-eighths from the exit or a quarter of the tunnel's length. If the train was to reach him at the exit, it would have to travel at four times John's speed, i.e. 40 miles per hour.

207. Red, White and Blue

There are six possible pairings of the two balls withdrawn:

RED + RED
RED + WHITE
WHITE + RED
RED + BLUE
BLUE + RED
WHITE + BLUE

We know that the WHITE + BLUE combination has not been drawn. This leaves five possible combinations remaining. Therefore the chances that the RED + RED pairing has been drawn are 1 in 5.

Many people cannot accept that the solution is not 1 in 3, and of course it would be, if the balls had been drawn out separately and the colour of the first ball announced as red before the second had been drawn out. However, as both balls had been drawn together, and then the colour of one of the balls announced, then the above solution, 1 in 5, must be the correct one.

208. Common Factor

Each word contains 3 consecutive letters from the alphabet.

209. Word Groups

The word DUNE from Group 2 belongs best with the words from Group 1, all of which may be preceded by the word "Sand."

210. Two Wins

If Bill is to win two games in a row, he must win the second game, so it is to his advantage to play that game against the weaker opponent. He must also win one game against the stronger opponent, and his chance is greater if he plays the stronger opponent twice. The first game should therefore be against his mother.

211. Find X

If each side is squared:

$$x+\sqrt{x+\sqrt{x+\sqrt{x}}}\ldots=4$$

and if, as is stated:

$$\sqrt{x+\sqrt{x+\sqrt{x}}}\ldots=2$$

then $x + 2 = 4$; so $x = 2$.

212. Pocketful of Coins

The lowest number of coins in a pocket is 0. The next greater number is at least 1, the next at least 2 and so on until the number in the ninth pocket is at least 9. Therefore the number of coins required is at least:

$$0+1+2+3+4+5+6+7+8+9=45$$

Since Freddy has only 44 coins, the answer is no.

213. Six-gallon Hat

The key is to reduce the content of container A to 6 gallons.

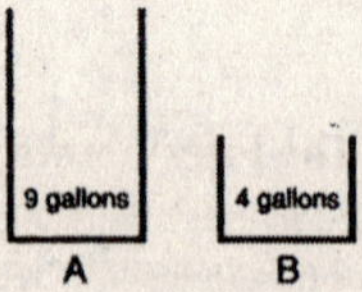

This can be achieved as follows:

1. Fill A.
2. Pour 4 gallons into B.
3. 5 gallons remain in A.
4. Empty B.
5. Refill B from A—this leaves 1 gallon in A.
6. Empty B and put the 1 gallon from A into B.
7. Refill A.
8. Fill B from A. This will take 3 gallons, leaving 6 in A.

214. Flock of Geese

We know each goose was sold for the same number of pounds as there were geese in the flock. If the number of geese is n, the total number of pounds received was n^2. This was paid in £10 notes plus an excess in coins. Since George drew both the first and last £10 notes, the number of £10 notes must have been odd, and since the square of any multiple of 10 contains an even number of tens, n must end in a digit, the square of which contains an odd number of tens. Only two digits, 4 and 6, have such squares: 16 and 36. Both squares end in 6, so n^2 is a number ending in 6. Thus the excess amount consisted of 6 pounds.

After Guy took the £6, he still had £4 less, so to even things up the older brother wrote out a cheque for £2.

215. Three Points on a Hemisphere

The probability is 1 (complete certainty). Any three points on a sphere must be on a hemisphere.

216. Deal a Bridge Hand

The dealer dealt the bottom card to himself, then continued dealing from the bottom anticlockwise.

217. The Fifty-pound Note

Since the counterfeit note was used in every transaction, they are all invalid. Therefore, everybody stands in the same position to his/her creditor as before the bank manager picked up the counterfeit note.

218. The Bicycle Race

12 minutes.

219. The North Pole

If West and East were stationary points, and West on your left when advancing towards North, then, after passing the Pole and turning around, West would be on your right. But West and East are not fixed points, but *directions* round the globe. So wherever you stand facing North, you will have the West direction on your left and East on your right.

220. Card Games

Nine. Jack wins 3 games and thus gains £3. Jill has to win back this £3, which takes another 3 games, then win a further 3 games.

221. Long-playing Record

About 3 inches. The needle moves from the outermost position to the center area of the label in an arc whose radius is the length of the pick-up arm.

222. Which Games?

One friend plays none of the games, so the other two must each play all three.

223. What Day Is It?

Today is Sunday.

The drawing below will assist:

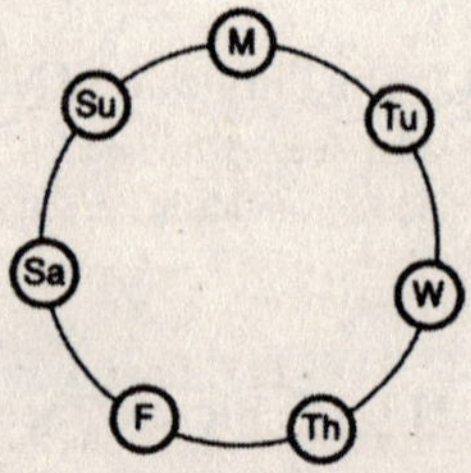

Choose a day at random, say Tuesday. Then:

1. When the day after tomorrow (Thursday) is yesterday (Monday), 4 days will have elapsed.
2. When the day before yesterday (Sunday) is tomorrow (Wednesday), 3 days will have elapsed.
3. Today will therefore be 7 days from Sunday; i.e. Sunday.

224. Cash Bags

The 10 bags should contain the following amounts: £1, £2, £4, £8, £16, £32, £64, £128, £256, £489.

225. Garage Space

Let the number of trucks be x. Then the garage had room for $(x - 8)$ trucks. By increasing the garage by 50 percent, there is now room for $(x + 8)$ trucks.

$$(x-8)+\frac{(x-8)}{2}=x+8$$

$$3(x-8)=2(x+8)$$

$$3x-24=2x+16$$

$$x=40$$

226. Bag of Chocolates

	Joan	*Jane*	*Jill*
	4 chocolates	3 chocolates	$\frac{14}{3}$ chocolates
or	12	9	14
Total	264	198	308
Ages	6	$4\frac{1}{2}$	7

227. Lost

Stand the signpost back up so that the arm indicating the place you just came from points in that direction. All the other arms will then point in the correct direction.

228. Problem Age

The statement was made on 1 January. Peter's birthday is 31 December. He was 17 the day before yesterday. Yesterday, the last day of last year, was his 18th birthday. He will be 19 on the last day of this year and 20 on the last day of next year.

229. Hex Sign

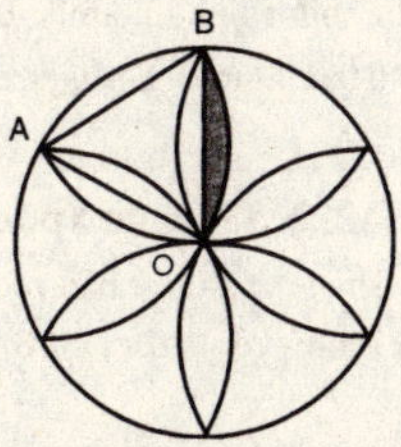

Let A and B be the end points of two neighbouring petals, and O the centre of the hex sign. Then AB = OA = OB = 1 centimetre.

We observe that half of one of the petals is equal to the difference between Δ ABO and the segment of a circle (see figure above).

The triangle is an equilateral triangle with sides equal to 1 centimetre. The area of such a triangle can be calculated by the formula ½ Base × Height.

Dropping a perpendicular line from one of the apexes to the middle of one of the sides, the height can be readily ascertained by the theory of Pythagoras to be:

$$\sqrt{(1)^2-(\tfrac{1}{2})^2}$$

and since the base is 1 cm, the area is

$$\tfrac{1}{2}\sqrt{1-\tfrac{1}{4}} - \tfrac{1}{4}\sqrt{3} = 0.433 \text{ square centimetres}$$

Turning to the segment of the circle in the right-hand illustration below, the angle at A is 60°, which is one sixth of 360°.

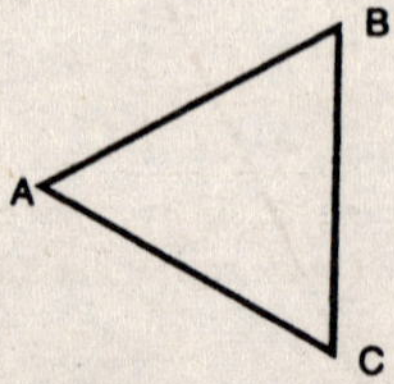

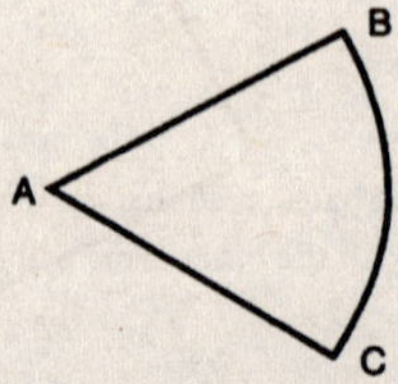

Therefore, the area of the segment is one sixth of the area of a circle with 1 centimetre radius or

$$\frac{\pi}{6} = 0.524 \text{ square centimetres}$$

The difference between these two areas is the area of half a petal.

Therefore, half a petal = 0.524 – 0.433

$$= 0.091 \text{ square centimetres}$$

and the area of a whole petal is 0.182 square centimetres.

230. Squares from a Square

By connecting the midpoint of each side with the corner opposite, we get 5 small squares, as shown.

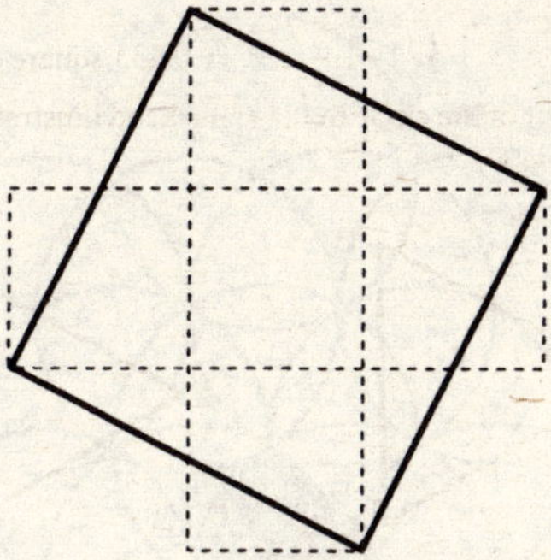

You will see from the diagram that the areas of the small squares add up to that of the large one. The triangles outside the square are congruent to the triangles inside the square.

231. The Goat

$\frac{3}{4}$ of original circle	=	1039.5	square feet
$\frac{1}{4}$ of circle, radius 14 feet	=	154.0	square feet
$\frac{1}{4}$ of circle, radius 7 feet	=	38.5	square feet
		1232.0	square feet
Original circle	=	1386.0	square feet
Grazing $^{1232}/_{1386}$	=	88.8% × $100	
Should pay		$88.80	
Reduction		$11.20	

232. Overlapping Circles

Three equal circles, each passing through the centres of the other two, can be repeated to form the pattern shown in the figure below.

Each circle is made up of 6 D shapes and 12 B shapes. One quarter of the area of a circle must therefore be equal to 1½ Ds plus 3 Bs. The area common to 3 mutually intersecting circles (shown shaded in the diagram) consists of 3 Bs and one D. Therefore it is smaller than a quarter of the area of a circle by an amount equal to half a D. In fact, the mutual overlap is just over 0.22 of the circle's area.

233. Sideways

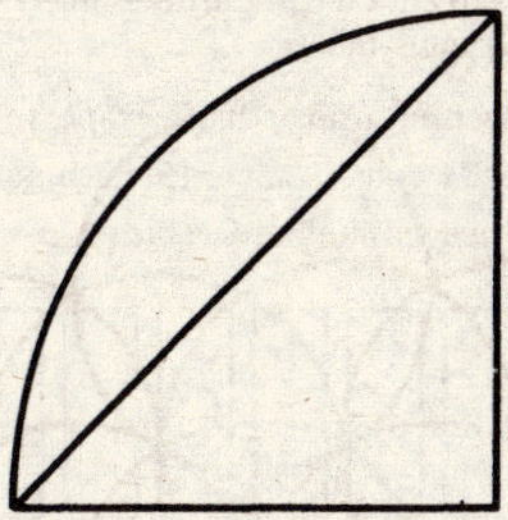

234. Spider and Fly

The shortest route the spider can walk to get to the fly is 40 feet. This is shown in the diagram of the unfolded room below. It is interesting to note that this route involves the spider walking across 5 of the room's 6 sides.

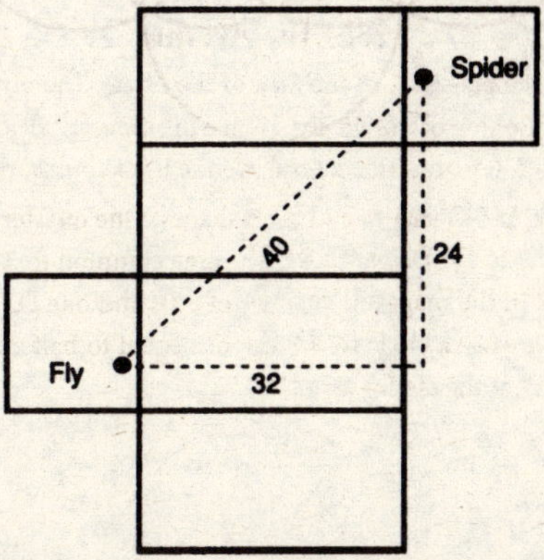

235. The Vanishing Square

The forger took 14 £20 notes and cut each of the notes into two parts as shown in the figure below (along the dotted lines).

He then stuck the upper section (using adhesive tape) to the appropriate section of the next note, with the result that 14 notes became 15. Each note was of course shortened by one-fifteenth of its length, which was not noticeable.

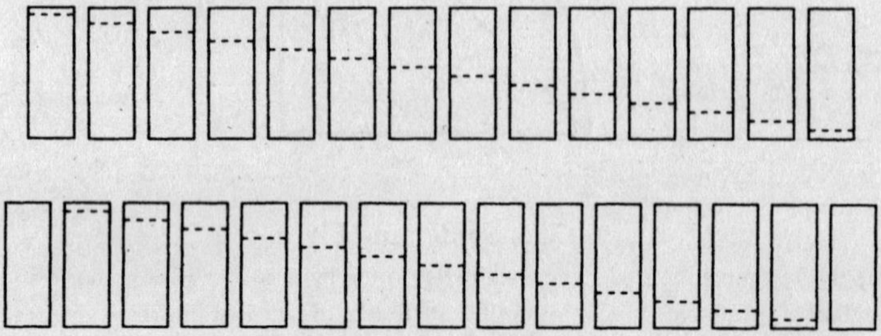

236. The Avenue

The area of the two triangles is $\frac{5}{12}$ of the area of the estate. Therefore the shortest side of each triangle is $\frac{5}{12}$ of the side of the square. Hence the longest side of each is $\frac{13}{12}$ of the side of the square, i.e. of 1,430 yards. The central avenue is, of course, the same length. So the central avenue is 1,430 yards long.

feet.